T0356033

SACRED UNIONS

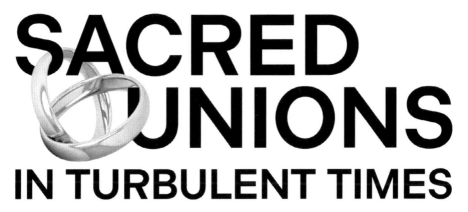

IN TURBULENT TIMES

The Ultimate Guide to Building and Sustaining a God-Honoring Marriage

DR. SHAUN T. CAMPBELL, DMFT

Sacred Unions in Turbulent Times

The Ultimate Guide to Building and Sustaining a God-Honoring Marriage

Dr. Shaun T. Campbell

ISBN: 979-8-35099-358-5

To my husband, Kavin

Who has been my unwavering source of support and encouragement in every endeavor I have pursued. Your presence in my life has been a constant reminder that I am never alone, no matter the challenges I face. Thank you for your patience, your prayers, your sacrifices, and the countless ways you've shown up for me, often without me even asking. I love you and I am eternally grateful for you, and I cherish the bond we share. You are my rock, my cheerleader, and my greatest blessing!

To my daughter, Taylor, and my son, Kristofor

Thank you for your love and the inspiration you provide to strive for excellence. Your confidence in my abilities has fueled my determination to push beyond limits and reach heights that have appeared overwhelming. Your faith in me is a treasure I hold dear, and your love has been a constant beacon, lighting my path.

To my beloved mother, the late Doris Jean Burks

Whose unwavering support and guidance have been instrumental in my covenant journey over the 35 years. Through both the joyful and challenging moments, you nurtured my sacred union with grace and strength, embodying the love and wisdom that have shaped my path.

CONTENTS

PART ONE:
Foundations of a God-Honoring Marriage

PART TWO:
Building Blocks for a Strong Marriage

PART THREE:
Strengthening Bonds

INTRODUCTION

In an era marked by uncertainty and rapid change, the sanctity of marriage faces unprecedented challenges. Couples are navigating turbulent waters, seeking to uphold the sacred union that reflects divine intention. "Sacred Unions in Turbulent Times" serves as a beacon for those striving to fortify their marital bonds amidst life's storms.

This book delves into the timeless principles that underpin a resilient, God-honoring marriage. Drawing inspiration from biblical teachings and contemporary insights, it offers practical guidance for couples to:

Deepen Spiritual Connection: Cultivate a shared faith that serves as the cornerstone of your relationship. By intentionally growing together in your spiritual walk, you establish a shared connection that influences how you handle challenges, celebrate victories, and make decisions as a couple.

Strengthen Commitment: Commitment is the backbone of a thriving marriage, and it requires intentional nurturing, especially when life's challenges test the bond between you and your spouse. Strengthening your commitment involves more than a verbal promise—it's a conscious decision to reaffirm your love, devotion, and dedication to one another through every season of life, including the difficult ones.

Enhance Communication: Effective communication is one of the most vital components of a healthy and enduring marriage. It serves as the bridge that connects two lives, allowing couples to share their thoughts, feelings, and aspirations openly while working through conflicts with grace and understanding. However, communication doesn't come naturally to every couple— it's a skill that requires intentionality, patience, and practice.

Foster Mutual Support: Mutual support is a necessity of a thriving marriage, where both individuals feel valued, heard, and cherished. It's about standing together as a team, offering encouragement, strength, and affirmation to one another in every season of life.

Through real-life stories, reflective exercises, and actionable steps, "Sacred Unions in Turbulent Times" empowers couples to transform challenges into opportunities for growth. It underscores the belief that, with faith and intentional effort, marriages will not only survive but thrive in challenging times, becoming a testament to enduring love and divine purpose.

My hope is that everyone who reads this material will be inspired, uplifted, and spiritually strengthened, gaining a renewed determination to surrender your marital covenant as a vessel in God's hands for His glory. It is my prayer that you grow in sensitivity to your spouse's needs and become increasingly aligned with God's divine purpose for your union.

Embark on this journey to strengthen the sacred union you share, building a flourishing bond that thrives with resilience and joy as you confidently embrace your tomorrows with faith and optimism.

PART ONE

*Foundations of a
God-Honoring Marriage*

Foundation of a Sacred Union

"Love is patient and kind. Love Is not jealous or boastful or proud or rude. It does not demand its own way. It is not irritable, and it keeps no record of being wronged. It does not rejoice about injustice but rejoices whenever the truth wins out. Love never gives up, never loses faith, is always hopeful, and endures through every circumstance." (1 Corinthians 13:4–7 NLT)

The sacred union between husband and wife becomes a steadfast anchor, grounding both partners in the strength of their faith despite life's challenges. A sacred union is deemed God-honoring because it is connected and dedicated to God for His glory and spiritual usage. Sacred unions are built on a foundation from the word of God, one that remains unshaken even in turbulent times. The beauty of this sacred bond, this divine covenant, is more than just a union between two people: it's a living reflection of the love and commitment between Christ and the Church. At the heart of such a marriage are three foundational pillars: love, sacrifice, and unity. These essential principles, deeply rooted in Scripture, set the tone for how a marriage can blossom amidst the complexities of life.

The first pillar of a sacred union is love (Agape) and this love goes far beyond emotions or temporary passion (Eros). Agape which is a selfless and unconditional love, embodies a deep, unwavering commitment to care for one another through every season of life—whether in moments of joy, during challenges, or when facing the mundane routines of everyday existence. This kind of love is not driven by fleeting feelings or circumstances but is rooted in choice and devotion. Spouses are intentional about maintaining the integrity and sanctity of their union. This type of love mirrors Christ's unconditional love for His people, a love that is steadfast, sacrificial, and enduring.

Within the confines of marriage, this means that both partners are called to prioritize each other above personal desires and convenience. It involves serving one another selflessly, putting the needs of your spouse above your own, and actively seeking to nurture the relationship even when life's pressures try to pull you apart. This love does not waver when times get hard— instead, it grows stronger through adversity, reflecting the faithfulness of Christ who remains constant in His commitment to us. When couples understand that love is a commitment to serve, honor, and sacrifice, they create a foundation that can withstand the trials and tests of life, drawing closer to each other and to God's perfect plan for their marriage.

The second pillar, sacrifice, stands in stark contrast to the culture around us where individualism and self-interest are often celebrated. In today's world, the idea of sacrificing personal desires for the benefit of another is often overlooked or undervalued. Yet, in a God-honoring marriage, sacrifice is at the very heart of the relationship. God calls couples to follow the example of Christ, who laid down His life for the world. For God so loved the world, that He gave, He sacrificed His only begotten Son because of that love (John 3:16). This type of selflessness is a way of life, a continual choice to put the needs of the spouse above one's own.

Sacrifice in marriage means choosing to let go of personal preferences and desires, even when it's not easy, in order to serve your partner. There have been many times when I've felt angry with Kav, yet I still chose to serve him. In those moments, serving him wasn't my first inclination, but I knew it was the right thing to do to honor God. Even when my feelings didn't align with my actions, I recognized that through sacrificing my own will to serve my husband, I was growing in my forgiveness quotient (FQ) and deepening my ability to love selflessly. Sacrifice is about offering patience in the face of frustration, kindness when irritation arises, and understanding when differences threaten to divide.

This sacrificial love creates an environment of grace where both partners feel secure in knowing that the other is willing to give for their well-being. Rather than causing division, sacrifice promotes healing and growth in a relationship. When both individuals are committed to serving one another and making sacrifices for the greater good of the marriage, the relationship is strengthened, and they can weather even the most difficult times together.

Unity is the third essential pillar of a sacred union, and it goes beyond physical togetherness or a shared space to encompass spiritual harmony. It's about aligning in faith, values, and purpose, with God at the center of the relationship. Spiritual unity draws a couple closer to each other and to God, forming a strong foundation that supports their relationship through life's challenges.

When couples pursue God together, seeking His guidance and aligning their lives with His will, they find strength and direction. This shared pursuit of God creates resilience in the marriage, enabling couples to face life's obstacles as a united front. Spiritual unity encourages both partners to grow individually while supporting one another in their faith journeys.

This unity doesn't erase our individual differences but embraces them within the context of a shared commitment to God's plan. In my marriage, Kav and I have learned that the goal isn't to pursue our own personal aspirations with the hope that God's word will simply align with our desires. Instead, true unity comes from knowing God's word, discerning His will for our marriage, and aligning ourselves with it to fulfill His purpose. Spiritual unity transforms the focus of the relationship from being "me" centered to "we" centered, helping both partners work together as a unified team with a common goal to honor God.

While a God-honoring marriage will certainly face trials, it stands firm by relying on God's truth, strength, and grace. When challenges come, this reliance on biblical principles provides the endurance necessary to persevere and come out stronger.

In the chapters ahead, we will explore each of these foundational pillars in greater depth, offering practical applications and biblical insights to help you cultivate a thriving, Christ-centered marriage that can stand the test of time.

CHAPTER 1

Devotion, Duty, and Divine Design:
A Biblical View of Marriage

In today's world, the shelves are packed with books and advice about marriage. You'll find everything from how to find "The One," to tips on reigniting passion, to steps for overcoming the inevitable ups and downs. Marriage can feel like a puzzle—one day, everything falls in place, and it feels like you and your spouse can take on the world. Then, out of nowhere, the winds shift, and you're left feeling misunderstood, distant, and frustrated. If you've been married for any length of time, you may have found yourself quietly wondering, "Why did I get married?"

In those challenging moments, it's easy to lose sight of the deeper purpose of marriage. Our culture often treats marriage like a trial-and-error process where if things don't work out, the solution is to walk away and try again—treating marriage like a discarded, ill-fitted jacket. However, God's design for marriage is far more enduring. He created marriage as a sacred duty, an unbreakable covenant, and not just a partnership of convenience. This chapter encourages us to look beyond fleeting emotions and cultural norms and instead embrace the profound, biblical foundation of marriage as a lifelong commitment. A sacred bond that endures not by ease or luck, but through devotion, faith, and love that mirrors God's own relationship with us.

Marriage as a Sacred Covenant

The biblical view of marriage as a "sacred union," a "God-honoring covenant," is deeply rooted in the very nature of God's relationship with humanity. A covenant is a solemn, binding agreement or promise between two parties. When we gave our lives to Christ, we entered an Everlasting Covenant that's not contractual in nature. God always keeps His end of the covenant, even when humanity dishonors theirs. Covenants supersede contracts because they are unconditional. In the Bible, marriage is a covenant—it's a divine, eternal institution entered into by three (the husband, the wife, and God) and designed to reflect the character of God's faithfulness, sacrifice, and love.

To describe the marital covenant as "sacred" highlights that marriage is not just a human agreement but one that involves God's presence and blessing. Too many couples are entering into marriage without understanding the spiritual implications. When husbands and wives stand at that altar to get married, God is present! God Himself is the ultimate witness of the vows exchanged at the wedding ceremony (Malachi 2:14), not our family and friends who sign the marriage certificate. God Himself is one of the three cords that fortify the marriage in Ecclesiastes 4:12. Viewing the marriage from this perspective elevates the union above companionship or how society socially constructs marriage to emphasizing the spiritual dimension of the relationship.

In Genesis 2:24, the creation of the first marriage between Adam and Eve establishes a profound understanding of the marital relationship. It says, "A man shall leave his father and his mother and hold fast to his wife, and they shall become one flesh." This verse not only defines marriage as a union of two individuals, but also speaks about the depth and sacred nature of that bond. The phrase "one flesh" signifies a deep unity that goes beyond physical connection—it encompasses emotional, spiritual, and relational oneness. Becoming one flesh is about the deep integration of lives, where the couple's desires, goals, and actions are aligned in a shared purpose.

Being "one flesh" signifies a deep unity that transcends physical intimacy, extending into emotional connections, shared responsibilities, mutual growth, and spiritual harmony. In the early years of our marriage, Kav and I didn't fully grasp the meaning of "one flesh." After our wedding, we continued to operate as two individuals with separate agendas. We often found ourselves in conflict, each trying to assert our own way. However, as we grew in our understanding of Jesus Christ, we began to recognize how important it was to align our individual desires with God's greater purpose for our marriage. We slowly learned to put our personal wants aside and seek His plan for our covenant, which ultimately strengthened our bond and brought us closer together.

My dream was to become a pediatrician, while Kavin's aspiration was to play professional basketball. I was an exceptional student, and he was a talented athlete. But when we united in marriage, we made the choice to set aside our individual ambitions and seek God's will for our lives, both personally and as a couple. God began to redirect our paths toward ministry, calling us to serve His people. As we embraced our roles as pastors, our desires, plans, and decisions began to align in a way that showed we were truly becoming "one flesh." While we understood the covenant aspect of marriage, it took time to fully embrace the concept of "one flesh" in this way. We no longer approached our marriage with a transactional mindset—"If you do this, I'll do that"—but instead, our love shifted to become more sacrificial and unconditional. We were now united in purpose, dedicated to the same mission, and our commitment to each other grew deeper as we walked this path together.

The Marital Covenant as a Symbol of Christ and the Church

Understanding marriage as a covenant between husband and wife lays the groundwork for grasping its deeper, spiritual significance. Many couples approach marriage from a purely human perspective, viewing it simply as a commitment between two people in an exclusive relationship. While this aspect is significant, marriage is far more profound than just an exclusive relationship between two. It is a sacred institution designed by God to serve as a living symbol of Christ's relationship with the Church, reflecting His selfless love, unwavering commitment, and redemptive purpose.

Just as a husband and wife pledge their love, faithfulness, and unity to one another, so too does Christ commit Himself to His bride, the Church, in an everlasting covenant of grace and redemption. By understanding this divine parallel, we can begin to see how marriage transcends earthly commitments. Marriage is a spiritual union that calls both partners to love, sacrifice, and serve in a way that mirrors Christ's love for His people.

In Ephesians 5:25–27, the Apostle Paul provides a profound comparison, urging husbands to love their wives "just as Christ loved the church and gave Himself up for her to make her holy, cleansing her by the washing with water through the word." While husbands cannot spiritually cleanse their wives (e.g., they cannot redeem them or sanctify them) like Jesus did for the Church, they can take an active role in supporting their wives' spiritual growth and well-being.

As the spiritual leaders of their homes, husbands have the responsibility to guide, nurture, and encourage their wives in their walk with God, creating an environment where holiness and devotion can flourish. By praying together, studying Scripture, and modeling Christ-like love, a husband fulfills his role as a spiritual protector, helping his wife remain aligned with God's will.

When marriage is viewed through this lens, it goes beyond the temporal and becomes a living testimony of God's covenantal love. Christ's unwavering commitment to His Church is marked by sacrifice, grace, and redemption. Similarly, the marital covenant calls husbands and wives to mirror these qualities. Wives are encouraged to submit to their husbands "as to the Lord" (Ephesians 5:22), and husbands are commanded to love their wives sacrificially. This mutual submission and love create a union that points back to the redemptive work of Christ.

Additionally, Revelation 19:7–9 refers to the Church as the bride of Christ, anticipating the ultimate union at the "wedding supper of the Lamb." This depiction highlights the divine significance of marriage as a symbol of the eternal relationship between Christ and His redeemed people. Just as the Church is called to prepare herself, remaining faithful and pure, so too are spouses called to nurture faithfulness, unity, and purity within their relationship.

Christ's sacrifice for the church and His ongoing commitment to sanctify and purify her (Ephesians 5:25–32) should be reflected in the way husbands and wives love and serve each other.

Ephesians 5:25–32 declares the following:

25 For husbands, this means love your wives, just as Christ loved the church. He gave up his life for her.

26 to make her holy and clean, washed by the cleansing of God's word.

27 He did this to present her to himself as a glorious church without a spot or wrinkle or any other blemish. Instead, she will be holy and without fault.

28 In the same way, husbands ought to love their wives as they love their own bodies. For a man who loves his wife shows love for himself.

29 No one hates his own body but feeds and cares for it, just as Christ cares for the church.

30 And we are members of his body.

31 As the Scriptures say, "A man leaves his father and mother and is joined to his wife, and the two are united into one."

32 This is a great mystery, but it is an illustration of the way Christ and the church are one.

In Ephesians 5:25, Paul exhorts husbands to love their wives as Christ loved the church and gave up His life for her. As briefly discussed, Paul used the Greek word Agape for love. The ancient Greeks had four different words that translated to love.

- *Eros* represents love driven by desire and passion, often associated with romantic and physical attraction. The term is the root of the word "erotic," reflecting its focus on intimacy and longing.

- *Storge* describes the natural affection shared within families, such as the love between parents and their children or the bond among siblings. It is a deep, instinctive connection rooted in familiarity, care, and shared experiences within the family unit.

- *Philia* refers to a love characterized by brotherly friendship and deep affection. It is the bond of close companionship and partnership, marked by shared interests, mutual respect, and genuine fondness. This type of love thrives in the context of meaningful connections, where individuals are united by common values and shared experiences.

Eros, Storge, and Philia—all speak of love that is felt. Love is bound by connection, desire, and friendship. These three types of love are extensions of the heart, and they are important in our relationships. But in the marriage, these three lower forms of love are not the foundation of this sacred union, but Agape, a higher love, is. It is a love more about intentionality and not based upon the sentiments of the heart. Agape love chooses to love the undeserving; it's intentional about its display and not predicated upon reciprocity. In this regard, Agape is not based upon feelings, and it has nothing to do with emotions—it is about denying oneself for the sake of another.

Eros, Storge, and Philia all describe love that is rooted in connection—love that stems from emotion, desire, or friendship. These expressions of love flow naturally from the heart and play an important role in human relationships, particularly in marriage. However, while these forms of love enrich the marital bond, they are not its foundation. The true foundation of a God-honoring marriage is "Agape," a higher, selfless love.

Agape love goes beyond feelings, making it essential for a thriving, God-honoring marriage. Too often, husbands and wives believe their marital roles and responsibilities are optional when emotions waver. For example, a husband may neglect helping around the house simply because he doesn't feel like it, or a wife might withhold intimacy because she isn't in the mood. These choices, driven by fleeting emotions, weaken the sacred union of marriage. Agape love calls both partners to rise above personal feelings, embracing an intentional and steadfast commitment to love and serve each other, even when it isn't convenient or seemingly deserved. This higher form of love is what sets a marriage apart as sacred and reflects what God originally intended.

Unlike emotional love, which can fluctuate with circumstances, Agape love is intentional and unwavering. It is not dependent on how the other person responds, but instead focuses on seeking the good of the other, rooted in sacrificial care and commitment. Agape is not driven by feelings, but by a conscious decision to put the needs of another before one's own. In marriage, this is the love the Apostle Paul is pointing husbands toward. This divine love serves as the foundation that upholds and strengthens the relationship, mirroring Christ's sacrificial love for His Church. It is through Agape love that couples are able to endure challenges and grow together, deepening their bond and reflecting God's unconditional love.

The divine parallel between husbands and wives, and Christ and the Church, changes the way we view marriage. It becomes more than just a partnership of "what's in it for me?"; it is a sacred calling to reflect the gospel to the world. Through daily acts of service, love, forgiveness, and sacrifice, couples have the unique opportunity within their union to demonstrate God's covenant with His people. This perspective not only elevates the purpose of marriage but also provides the strength and clarity to face its challenges with grace and hope.

Ultimately, the spiritual significance of marriage lies in its ability to glorify God. When couples prioritize their relationship with Him, by being doers of the word and not just hearers only, their love for each other becomes a testimony of His favor and power. A God-honoring marriage is a ray of hope in a world that often devalues commitment, serving as a witness to the beauty of living according to our Heavenly Father's design.

By embracing the spiritual dimensions of marriage, couples can experience a deeper sense of purpose, unity, and fulfillment, knowing that their union is part of a greater divine plan.

Warning Against Ungodly Covenants
Malachi 2:11–16

11 Judah has been unfaithful, and a detestable thing has been done in Israel and in Jerusalem. The men of Judah have defiled the Lord's beloved sanctuary by marrying women who worship idols.

12 May the Lord cut off from the nation of Israel every last man who has done this and yet brings an offering to the Lord of Heaven's Armies.

13 Here is another thing you do, You cover the Lord's altar with tears, weeping, and groaning because he pays no attention to your offerings and doesn't accept them with pleasure.

14 You cry out, "Why doesn't the LORD accept my worship?" I'll tell you why! Because the LORD witnessed the vows you and your wife made when you were young. But you have been unfaithful to her, though she remained your faithful partner, the wife of your marriage vows.

15 Didn't the LORD make you one with your wife? In body and spirit, you are his. And what does he want? Godly children from your union. So guard your heart; remain loyal to the wife of your youth.

16 "For I hate divorce!" says the LORD, the God of Israel. "To divorce your wife is to overwhelm her with cruelty," says the LORD of Heaven's Armies. "So guard your heart; do not be unfaithful to your wife."

You might be wondering, "What does the book of Malachi have to do with marriage?" Well, beloved, Malachi speaks directly to marriage and God's intent to protect and honor this sacred institution. In the second chapter, Malachi addresses the unfaithfulness of the priests, revealing their actions and how God exposes their disobedience.

God's complaint against the priests in Malachi was twofold. First, they strayed from God's ways and caused many to stumble in their understanding of the law. Secondly, God condemned the priests for their treachery, particularly in how they handled their marriages. Let's take a closer look at the latter issue and explore marriage from a biblical perspective.

Malachi 2:11 says, "The men of Judah have defiled the Lord's beloved sanctuary by marrying women who worship idols." King James Version states, "for Judah hath profaned the holiness of the Lord which he loved, and hath married the daughter of a strange god."

This verse highlights a significant spiritual principle: the danger of being unequally yoked in relationships, particularly in the covenant of marriage. The men of Judah had "defiled the Lord's beloved sanctuary" or "profaned the holiness of the Lord" by marrying women who worshiped idols—women who did not share their faith or commitment to the one true God. This act wasn't just a matter of personal preference or cultural integration; it represented a direct violation of God's covenant and a betrayal of His love for His people. Spiritually, this choice weakened their relationship with God and threatened the collective holiness of the nation.

From a biblical perspective, being unequally yoked means entering into a partnership where one person's values, beliefs, and spiritual commitments are fundamentally at odds with the others. As we previously established, marriage, as a sacred covenant, is intended to reflect God's relationship with His people—a relationship rooted in unity, love, and shared purpose. When one spouse is devoted to God and the other is devoted to idols or incompatible beliefs, it creates a spiritual dissonance that disrupts the harmony and sanctity of the marriage.

In this context, the men of Judah were not just defiling themselves but also dishonoring the covenant community and the Lord Himself. Their actions showed a disregard for God's commandments and a lack of reverence for the spiritual significance of marriage. By marrying "the daughter of a strange god," they symbolically invited idolatry and compromise into their homes and families, which could have extensive consequences for future generations. This was not simply a personal failure; it was also a communal and spiritual one.

The New Testament highlights this principle in 2 Corinthians 6:14, which warns believers not to be "unequally yoked with unbelievers." This isn't a condemnation of those outside the faith but rather a call for believers to align their most intimate relationships with God's will. Marriage is more than companionship; it is a spiritual partnership designed to glorify God. When spouses are unequally yoked, their values and goals often conflict, making it difficult to pursue a unified vision for their lives, including raising children in the faith, serving in ministry, or growing in spiritual maturity.

Spiritually, being unequally yoked introduces division where there should be unity. Instead of a marriage where both partners encourage each other to draw closer to God, the differing spiritual priorities can lead to compromise, frustration, or even alienation from God. For example, a Christian mother's goal for her children is for them to know and follow Christ, teaching them to pray, read the Bible, and attend church. However, her husband, who is indifferent or adheres to another belief system, may resist these practices or promote a conflicting worldview. This can confuse the children and strain the marriage as the parents clash over foundational values.

Sometimes, a Christian couple can be unequally yoked as one is more spiritually advanced and mature than the other. A husband might feel called to serve in church leadership or missionary work, requiring significant time and effort. Whereas his spouse, who isn't as involved or committed to the ministry, might view this as an unnecessary burden on their marriage or family life, leading to feelings of resentment or neglect. Both are believers, both attend the same ministry, yet their commitments are not compatible.

The story of Judah's unfaithfulness in Malachi reminds us that choices in marriage have profound spiritual consequences, not just for the individuals involved but also for the larger community of faith. Being unequally yoked can hinder unity, disrupt spiritual growth, and create emotional and relational strain. In contrast, when both spouses share a similar commitment to Christ, they can work through challenges together with shared faith and values, leading to a deeper connection and a stronger, God-honoring marriage.

To honor God's design for marriage, believers are called to seek partners who share their faith as well as their commitment to Him. This unity allows the couple to grow together in faith, order their lives with God's purpose, and reflect His love and glory through their covenant. Judah's failure serves as a cautionary tale about the spiritual risks of prioritizing personal desires over God's will in the sacred institution of marriage.

There are examples in the Bible that address the dangers of ungodly covenants:

- **Numbers 25 (Israel married women from Moab)**
  While the Israelites were camped at Acacia Grove, some of the men defiled themselves by having sexual relations with local Moabite women. These women invited them to attend sacrifices to their gods, so the Israelites feasted with them and worshiped the gods of Moab. In this way, Israel joined in the worship of Baal of Peor causing the Lord's anger to blaze against his people. (Numbers 25:1–3)

- **1 Kings 11 (Solomon married foreign women)**
  Now King Solomon loved many foreign women. Besides Pharaoh's daughter, he married women from Moab, Ammon, Edom, Sidon, and from among the Hittites. The Lord had clearly instructed the people of Israel, "You must not marry them, because they will turn your hearts to their gods." Yet Solomon insisted on loving them anyway. (1 Kings 11:1–2)

- **1 Kings 16 (Ahab married Jezebel)**
  Ahab son of Omari began to rule over Israel in the thirty-eighth year of King Asa's reign in Judah. He reigned in Samaria for twenty-two years. But Ahab son of Omari did what was evil in the Lord's sight, even more than any of the kings before him. And as though it were not enough to follow the example of Jeroboam, he married Jezebel, the daughter of King Ethbaal of the Sidonians, and he began to bow down in worship of Baal. (1 Kings 16:29–31)

In these marriages, God's servants entered covenants with women who did not honor Him, as demonstrated by the introduction of idolatry into their homes. This occurred when they married outside their faith, not outside their race. God took issue with this back then, and He still takes issue with it today. In Malachi 2:12, God warns that He will punish the priests who acted in this way, thinking they could continue offering sacrifices as if nothing was wrong. This was a serious breach of their covenant with God, and He would not overlook it. The message here is clear: God values faithfulness in marriage and expects His people to honor Him in every aspect of their lives, including their relationships.

Results of Dishonoring the Marital Covenant

Malachi 2:13 declares, "Here is another thing you do. You cover the Lord's altar with tears, weeping and groaning because he pays no attention to your offerings and doesn't accept them with pleasure."

> In this passage, we find the priests weeping at the altar, lamenting because God is not accepting their offerings. There are times when our offerings are considered unacceptable before God. In verse 13, the Scripture reveals that God does not pay attention to our offerings, and in verse 14, it explains why.

Malachi 2:14 reiterates, "You cry out, 'Why doesn't the Lord accept my worship?' I'll tell you why! Because the Lord witnessed the vows you and your wife made when you were young. But you have been unfaithful to her, though she remained your faithful partner, the wife of your marriage vows."

> The Lord did not accept the priest's worship in giving specifically because of his unfaithfulness to his wife. Infidelity violates the sacredness of the marriage. The Scripture tells us that this type of maltreatment of one's spouse, particularly the wife in this context, is grounds for God rejecting our offerings, regardless of our tears, begging, and pleading. This shows that our financial health and blessings are directly connected to how we honor our marriage. If God does not accept our offerings, it impacts the harvest we receive. Ultimately, God desires true faithfulness and righteousness in our marriages over mere religious rituals or outward acts. Our

relationship with our spouse reflects our relationship with God, and He calls us to honor this covenant above all else.

God is not moved by empty acts of worship when there is a lack of genuine faithfulness in the marriage covenant. Many couples may appear spiritually active. They may faithfully attend church, give offerings, or serve in ministry, yet they neglect the core responsibilities within their marriage. Actions such as harboring resentment, being unfaithful, or failing to make your spouse a priority, dishonors the covenant and displease God. He looks beyond surface-level displays and desires a heart that is fully committed to the sacred union of marriage, that lines up with His principles of love, forgiveness, and unity.

Malachi 2:15 asks, "Didn't the Lord make you one with your wife? In body and spirit, you are his. And what does he want? Godly children from your union. So, guard your heart—remain loyal to the wife of your youth.

In this verse, the Lord asks a profound question: "Didn't the Lord make you one with your wife?" This rhetorical question once again emphasizes the oneness of marriage that was spoken of in Genesis 2:24. In body and spirit, the couple belongs to God. The union is a sacred partnership, one where both individuals are entrusted with the responsibility of nurturing each other and honoring God in their relationship.

The verse goes further, revealing God's desire for godly offspring from this union. This highlights that marriage is also about the legacy they create together. The children that come from such a union are meant to be raised in an environment that reflects God's love, teaching, and faithfulness. This is why it is so vital for spouses to nurture their marriage with loyalty, commitment, and faithfulness. The fruit of this union results in a strong and loving relationship between the husband and wife as well as the godly example they provide for their children.

Malachi 2:16 emphatically declares, "For I hate divorce!" Says the Lord, the God of Israel. "To divorce your wife is to overwhelm her with cruelty," says the Lord of Heaven's Armies. "So, guard your heart; do not be unfaithful to your wife."

> This is very clear—God hates divorce! He hates divorce because it destroys something sacred that He cherishes, and that's marriage— God's holy institution. From a biblical view, sacred vows are made before God and divorce undermines the covenantal commitment that is meant to be lifelong. God hates divorce because it causes deep harm, leaving lasting emotional and spiritual damage not only to the couple but also to their families and supporters. Divorce ultimately symbolizes spiritual unfaithfulness, reflecting a severing of the covenant with God.

Biblical View of Marital Submission

The Bible presents a balanced and nuanced view of submission within marriage. In passages like Ephesians 5:22–33, the Apostle Paul outlines a model for how a husband and wife should relate to each other in the context of Christian marriage.

Paul instructs wives to "submit to your own husbands, as to the Lord" (Ephesians 5:22). This submission is not about inferiority but about respect and honoring the role of leadership God has given to the husband within the family. It reflects a willingness to cooperate and follow the husband's lead as he seeks to guide the family in a Christ-like manner.

Equally, if not more challenging, is Paul's call for husbands to love their wives "as Christ loved the church and gave Himself up for her" (Ephesians 5:25). This means husbands are called to lead through sacrificial love, prioritizing the well-being of their wives above their own desires. True biblical leadership is not domineering but selfless and protective, mirroring Christ's love for His people.

The Bible also emphasizes mutual submission in godly marriages. Ephesians 5:21 says, "Submit to one another out of reverence for Christ." This call to mutual submission means that both spouses are called to humility, putting each other's needs and well-being first, which cultivates harmony and love in the relationship. When a husband serves his wife and a wife serves her husband, selfishness cannot find expression in that marriage. The act of serving each other dismantles self-centered tendencies, replacing them with a mindset of sacrificial love. In this dynamic, there's no need for self-serving behavior because each spouse is dedicated to meeting the other's needs.

Challenges to Mutual Submission

In modern society, honoring mutual submission is challenging for several reasons.

Selfishness

Society often emphasizes personal freedom, autonomy, and self-interest. In contrast, mutual submission calls for selflessness, putting others' needs ahead of one's own. For many, this goes against the dominant discourse that promotes "looking out for number one." The cultural narrative suggests that putting someone else first might result in a loss of personal power or identity.

For example, a couple might struggle with decision-making, where both feel that their personal preferences should come first. When Apostle and I married in our teenage years, this was definitely an issue because we didn't understand mutual respect and submission. I didn't want to give up my way for his and vice versa. When this happens in a marriage, instead of working together in love and sacrifice, couples are likely to compete for control, causing tension in the relationship.

Perceived Loss of Control

Submission, especially in marriage, is often misunderstood as being synonymous with weakness or oppression. In a world that often equates power with dominance, the biblical concept of submission, where love, service, and sacrifice are at the center, is often rejected. People tend to resist the idea of submission because it is seen as a loss of control, rather than an expression of love and respect.

A husband might feel the need to assert his authority in a dominant or controlling manner, thinking that if he leads with gentleness and sacrificial love, he will be perceived as weak or ineffective. Society often equates strength with control, so he may worry that a more compassionate approach could undermine his role as the leader of the family. As a result, he may lean toward harshness to feel secure in his authority, rather than leading in the humble, Christ-like way the Bible encourages.

On the other hand, a wife might resist the idea of submission because it can be misunderstood as subservience or losing her voice in the marriage. Instead of viewing submission as a voluntary and respectful partnership, where both spouses work together in love, she might see it as giving up her independence or being reduced to a lesser role. This misunderstanding can create tension, as she struggles to balance her desire for equality with the biblical call for mutual respect and cooperation in the marriage.

In both cases, the cultural pressures and misconceptions about power, leadership, and submission create barriers to the healthy, loving dynamic that God intended for marriage. For a husband, this means overcoming the fear of appearing weak and embracing servant leadership. For a wife, it means recognizing that biblical submission is about unity and respect, not inferiority or passivity. Together, both must work to redefine their roles in a way that honors each other and reflects Christ's example of humility and love.

Subscribing to Modern Relationship Approaches

In many parts of the world, gender roles are changing rapidly. While the Bible's concept of submission is based on mutual respect and different, but complementary roles within marriage, modern ideas about gender often blur these distinctions, leading to confusion or outright rejection of biblical marital roles (Marital Roles will be addressed in greater detail in chapter three).

In a marriage where both spouses have equally demanding careers, the traditional distinctions between husband and wife roles may become blurred. With both partners juggling professional responsibilities, the expectation of who should take charge in certain areas of family life, such as decision-making, household management, or child-rearing, can become unclear. This can lead to confusion and tension as each spouse might feel overwhelmed by their work obligations and uncertain about how to navigate their roles at home.

For example, a couple may struggle with the question of who should lead in managing finances or overseeing family decisions when both are equally contributing to the household income. Without clear guidance or communication, these blurred roles can result in frustration or a sense of imbalance. One partner may begin to feel that they are carrying an unfair share of the household responsibilities, while the other might feel undermined or unappreciated for what they contribute to the family.

Furthermore, in these situations, the concept of submission can be easily misunderstood. The wife, for instance, may feel that because she is just as involved in the professional world, the idea of submission is outdated or irrelevant. She may associate submission with the idea of being subservient or less capable, particularly when both partners are equally involved in providing for the family. On the other hand, the husband may feel unsure about how to lead in the marriage without coming across as domineering, especially when both are sharing similar pressures and responsibilities.

The challenge here is that modern career demands can make it harder for couples to understand and embrace the biblical model of mutual submission. Both partners must work together to redefine their roles in a way that honors the unique contributions each makes, both inside and outside the home. It requires intentional communication, a shared vision for the marriage, and a willingness to submit to each other in love and humility, recognizing that leadership and submission are not about who works more or earns more but about promoting unity and harmony within the relationship.

<u>Fear of Vulnerability</u>

True submission in marriage requires vulnerability and trust. Many people, due to past experiences or fear of being hurt, find it difficult to entrust their spouse with leadership or to genuinely serve and submit in love. This lack of trust can create a barrier to the deep unity that God intends for marriage.

Vignette

Joan had grown up in a home where control was the norm. Her father ruled the household with a heavy hand, making all the decisions without consulting her mother. Joan often saw the pain in her mother's eyes, the quiet resignation as she went along with whatever her father decided. It wasn't that her mother lacked opinions or desires—it was that they didn't matter. Joan vowed that her marriage would be different. She promised herself that she'd never allow someone else to control her, especially not her husband.

Years later, Joan married Daniel, a man who deeply loved God and strived to lead his family according to biblical principles. Daniel wasn't like Joan's father. He wasn't domineering or manipulative. In fact, he made a genuine effort to honor Joan in every decision, always seeking to include her thoughts and feelings. But despite his loving nature, she struggled to fully trust his leadership. Every time Daniel made a decision for their family, a voice in the back of Joan's mind warned her to be careful, to hold onto control so she wouldn't end up like her mother, silent and sidelined.

Daniel could sense Joan's reluctance. It seemed like no matter how much he tried to lead with love and care, she always kept a bit of distance, second-guessing his decisions or asserting her own opinions forcefully. He didn't understand why she seemed so guarded when all he wanted was what was best for both of them. Daniel began to feel frustrated. He wanted to lead the way the Bible taught him, but Joan's resistance made him doubt himself. Was he doing something wrong, or was there something deeper at play?

On the other hand, Daniel had his own internal battle. Growing up, he'd been taught that leadership meant taking charge, being decisive, and not relying too much on others. His father had always been the one to make the big decisions in the family, and while he didn't want to repeat that exact model, he sometimes found it hard to listen to Joan's advice. Her suggestions often felt like challenges to his authority, even though he knew deep down that wasn't her intention. When Joan would offer her perspective, Daniel felt an uncomfortable knot tighten in his chest. What if listening to her made him seem weak? What if her ideas somehow undermined his ability to lead?

One evening, the tension came to a head. They had been discussing how to manage their finances. Joan wanted to set aside more money for savings, while Daniel felt they needed to invest more in their home. The conversation, which started calmly, quickly spiraled into an argument.

"You never trust me to lead," Daniel blurted out, frustration evident in his voice. "I'm trying to do what's best for us, but it feels like you're always questioning everything I do."

Joan, equally upset, shot back, "It's not that I don't trust you, Daniel! It's just . . . I've seen what happens when someone has too much control. I'm not going to be like my mother, sitting on the sidelines with no say in our lives."

Her words had a lingering effect, and the tension grew heavier with the weight of unspoken fears and past wounds.

Daniel paused, realizing for the first time that Joan's resistance wasn't about him. It was about the patterns she had grown up with, the ones that had shaped her understanding of marriage and leadership. He reached out and gently took her hand.

"I'm not your father, Joan," he said softly. "I don't want to control you. I want us to lead together. But I need you to trust me, just like I need to learn to trust your advice. I don't want to make decisions alone."

Joan's eyes welled up with tears, the walls she had built around her heart beginning to crumble. She realized that Daniel's leadership wasn't like her father's. He wasn't trying to silence her—he was trying to love her. She also saw how her own fears had kept her from fully trusting him, even when he had shown nothing but care and respect.

"I do trust you," she whispered. "I'm just . . . scared. Scared of what I saw growing up and scared of losing myself in the process."

Daniel nodded, understanding her fear in a way he hadn't before. "I don't want you to lose yourself. Your voice matters, Joan. We're in this together. I need your input just as much as you need mine."

In that moment, they both saw what had been missing. Daniel needed to embrace Joan's counsel without feeling threatened, and Joan needed to let go of her past fears, trusting that Daniel's leadership wasn't about control, but about love. Both of them realized that true biblical submission and leadership weren't about power, but about partnership—working together in humility and grace, honoring each other's roles while seeking God's direction for their marriage.

It wasn't going to be easy, but for the first time in a long time, they felt hopeful. They had uncovered the root of their struggle, and with that understanding, they could begin to build the marriage God intended for them—a relationship based on mutual trust, sacrificial love, and shared leadership.

Mutual submission in marriage, as described in the Bible, is about loving sacrificially, respect, and partnership. Both the husband and wife are called to serve one another in ways that reflect Christ's love for the church. While this ideal is beautiful, it is hard to live out in today's society due to competing values like individualism, misunderstandings of authority, shifting gender roles, and a fear of vulnerability. Nevertheless, when a couple strives to live according to this biblical model, they create a relationship rooted in love, selflessness, and unity, reflecting a biblical view of marriage.

In Ephesians 5:22, wives are called to submit to their husbands as to the Lord. Verse 24 reiterates the wives' submission as it states, "As the church submits to Christ, so you wives should submit to your husbands in everything."

Paul's call for wives to submit to their husbands (Ephesians 5:22) should be understood in the context of mutual submission

(Ephesians 5:21), where both spouses are called to put the other's needs and well-being above their own.

Biblical Examples of Sacrificial Love in Marriage

Abraham and Sarah

Abraham and Sarah's story is a profound example of sacrificial love and trust in God's promises. When God called Abraham to leave his homeland and journey to an unknown destination, it was not only a test of his faith but also of Sarah's commitment. Sarah willingly left behind her family, security, and everything familiar to follow Abraham into uncertainty, exemplifying the unity and partnership central to a God-honoring marriage.

Their shared sacrifices were significant. From enduring famine to waiting decades for the fulfillment of God's promise of a son, their faith was tested repeatedly. Though Sarah sometimes doubted, as seen in her initial disbelief about bearing a child in old age, she remained by Abraham's side, showing that sacrificial love perseveres even when circumstances seem impossible.

Abraham's protective love for Sarah demonstrated his deep care and responsibility for her well-being. When they faced potential threats in foreign lands, such as in Egypt and with King Abimelech, Abraham took steps (not necessarily the best) to shield Sarah from harm. These moments reveal a husband's role in guarding his wife and reflect a love that seeks her safety and well-being.

Through their journey, Abraham and Sarah learned to trust God together, growing in faith and unity. Their story reminds us that sacrificial love in marriage will be filled with challenges, trust in God's faithfulness, and prioritizing each other's well-being.

Jacob and Rachel

Jacob's love for Rachel is a profound example of enduring and sacrificial love. When he first met her, he was so captivated that he willingly agreed to work seven years for her father, Laban, as the bride price. Yet, after being deceived into marrying her sister Leah, Jacob's love for Rachel did not waver. He committed to another seven years of labor to fulfill his promise and marry the woman he loved. This unyielding determination showcases a love that goes beyond immediate gratification, embracing patience, persistence, and sacrifice. Jacob's commitment reflects a deeper understanding of love as an intentional choice rather than a fleeting emotion. His willingness to give up years of his life and labor to be with Rachel serves as a timeless reminder of the power of steadfast love and dedication in the face of challenges.

Hosea and Gomer

One of the most profound examples of sacrificial love in marriage is found in the story of Hosea and Gomer (Hosea 1–3). In this narrative, God commands the prophet Hosea to marry Gomer, a woman who would repeatedly be unfaithful to him. Despite her continual betrayals, Hosea's love for Gomer never wavers, and he chooses to take her back again and again. This difficult and painful marriage is meant to be a living parable of God's unwavering love for Israel, who, like Gomer, had strayed and been unfaithful to God. Hosea's sacrificial love for Gomer illustrates the kind of love God demonstrates toward us—persistent, forgiving, and steadfast, even when we fall short.

In a similar way, Hosea's story serves as a powerful reminder of the depth of love and forgiveness that marriage often requires. In any relationship, especially marriage, there will be times of hardship, disappointment, and even betrayal. Yet, just as Hosea was called to remain faithful and loving, we too are called to love and serve our spouses even in difficult circumstances. This doesn't mean accepting harmful behavior without boundaries, but it does mean embracing the kind of grace and commitment that mirrors God's own love for us. Hosea's willingness to forgive and restore his relationship with Gomer is a picture of the sacrificial love that can transform and redeem a marriage, even when it feels beyond repair.

Boaz and Ruth

Another powerful example of love and commitment is found in the story of Ruth and Boaz. Ruth's devotion to her mother-in-law, Naomi, after the death of her husband is a powerful picture of loyalty and selflessness. Despite her own grief and uncertain future, Ruth chooses to stay with Naomi, declaring, "Where you go, I will go," and takes on the responsibility of caring for her. Ruth's decision to leave her homeland and embrace an unknown future in Bethlehem is a testament to her sacrificial love and willingness to put the needs of others before her own. Her actions embody the kind of commitment and faithfulness that is essential in any healthy marriage.

When Ruth meets Boaz, we see how her loyalty and kindness are met with honor and respect. Boaz, recognizing Ruth's character, responds not only with generosity but with a protective and caring love. He goes out of his way to ensure Ruth's safety and well-being, eventually becoming her kinsman-redeemer. Their relationship is a beautiful picture of how love rooted in service, respect, and mutual care forms the foundation of a godly marriage. Ruth's selflessness and Boaz's integrity reflect the kind of love that seeks to uplift, protect, and prioritize the well-being of the other—qualities that are vital to a thriving, Christ-centered relationship. Their story teaches us that a marriage built on kindness, loyalty, and a willingness to put others first can flourish even in the face of adversity.

Joseph and Mary

Joseph's decision to marry Mary, despite the extraordinary circumstances of her pregnancy, is a powerful demonstration of sacrificial love. When Joseph discovered that Mary was pregnant, he initially planned to divorce her quietly to spare her public disgrace, showing compassion even before understanding the divine nature of her situation. However, after an angel appeared to him in a dream and revealed that the child was conceived by the Holy Spirit, Joseph obediently embraced his role as husband to Mary and earthly father to Jesus. This decision required immense personal sacrifice, as Joseph faced potential social stigma and judgment from his community. Despite these challenges, he provided for Mary and protected her, demonstrating unwavering love and commitment. Joseph's actions reflect a love rooted in faith, obedience, and selflessness, serving as a profound example of how sacred unions can survive turbulent times.

Chapter Reflections

A biblical view of marriage as a symbol of Christ's relationship with the church redefines its purpose from personal fulfillment to mutual service and sacrifice. Considering this, marriage transcends the worldly notion of companionship, becoming a deep, spiritual partnership where both spouses seek to honor God by loving and serving each other selflessly. This type of commitment embodies a spiritual unity that glorifies God and deepens the couple's union.

In the creation narrative, marriage is established as a foundational element of God's design for humanity, demonstrating its significance in the divine order. Genesis 2:24 provides the key framework for understanding marriage: "Therefore a man shall leave his father and his mother and hold fast to his wife, and they shall become one flesh." This verse expresses the essence of marriage as a union that is both exclusive and profound, requiring a deliberate reordering of relational priorities.

For many spouses who are enmeshed in their families of origin, breaking away to honor the marriage over that initial family unit is often misunderstood as an act of betrayal. However, Scripture is clear in its directive to "leave one's father and mother and cleave unto the wife." The concept of "leaving and cleaving" signifies the transition from the primary familial bond with one's parents to an unbreakable, intimate bond with one's spouse. Unfortunately, this is why many husbands and wives struggle to become one flesh because they have not reordered their relational priorities. Ultimately, "leaving and cleaving" goes beyond physical separation, and it extends to a profound spiritual commitment that redefines the nature of all other relationships.

The instruction to "join" to one's spouse (Genesis 2:24b) emphasizes the covenantal nature of marriage, where both partners are called to loyalty and devotion. This bond is meant to be inviolable, transcending all other human connections. However, marriages often face challenges when external relationships—whether with children, parents, in-laws, or friends—intrude upon this sacred dyad. Such external influences can create tension and division, threatening the unity and harmony that marriage is intended to nurture and protect.

In this light, marriage is not a static institution but a dynamic journey of faith, where two individuals walk together, striving to reflect God's love not only in their relationship but also in their family and community. The marital covenant is a space where both partners are called to mutual edification, encouraging one another to grow in faith and character, thereby strengthening the bond between them.

Grounding a marriage in these biblical principles creates a robust foundation capable of withstanding the inevitable trials and challenges of life. As couples prioritize their relationship with each other and with God, they cultivate a partnership that is resilient, fulfilling, and reflective of the divine love that inspired its creation. The journey toward a God-honoring marriage begins with a deep understanding and embrace of this spiritual perspective, recognizing that marriage, at its core, is a sacred reflection of God's eternal commitment to His people.

Prayer

Heavenly Father,

We come before You as one, united in the sacred bond of marriage that You have designed and blessed. In these turbulent times, when challenges press upon us from every side, we seek Your divine protection and guidance to keep our union strong and centered in Your divine plan for our covenant.

When the pressures of the world threaten our marriage, remind us of the sacred covenant we made before You. Help us to anchor ourselves in Your

Word, which assures us that a three-fold cord is not easily broken. Draw us ever closer to You, Lord, so that in Your presence, we may be drawn closer to each other.

In Jesus' name, we pray, Amen.

CHAPTER 2

Dedication, Deference, and Dependability:
The Importance of Commitment

"And may your hearts be fully committed to the Lord our God, to live by his decrees and obey his commands, as at this time."

(1 Kings 8:61, NIV)

Dedication is one of the foundational pillars of a God-honoring, sacred union. It is the unwavering promise to love, honor, and cherish one's spouse through all seasons of life. This level of commitment mirrors God's unconditional love for us—a love that is steadfast, forgiving, and enduring. True dedication involves a commitment that manifests in consistent actions that demonstrate care, loyalty, and deference for one's partner. It is through this mutual respect that couples create an environment where love can flourish, and where dependability builds the trust needed to weather every trial.

This sacred dedication is not just a private vow but a transformative shift in priorities and relationships. In a world where relationships can be easily discarded after difficulties arise, an enduring sacred union stands as a testament to the power of commitment and dependability. This commitment includes the willingness to leave the familiar structures of the family of origin and embracing a new unified family system (nuclear family), as described in Genesis 2:24: "Therefore shall a man leave his father and his mother and shall cleave unto his wife: and they shall be one flesh." This act of cleaving requires both deference for the individuality of one's spouse and the dependability to uphold their needs as a priority within God's design for marriage.

In Genesis 2, the Bible lays the groundwork for a God-honoring marriage providing demonstrable steps that set the stage for success. Before Adam and Eve were united, God assigned Adam the responsibility of tending the Garden of Eden. This commitment was foundational, demonstrating Adam's accountability to God and his readiness to steward creation. Before introducing a woman into Adam's life, God ensured Adam was committed to his divine purpose, reflecting his ability to honor God through diligent work. Adam's responsibility to tend the garden was a test of his capacity to manage, provide, and lead—a prerequisite for his future role as a husband.

God's design underscores an important principle: if a man cannot honor God in his individual purpose, he is unlikely to honor his wife within the covenant of marriage. Only after Adam fulfilled his initial responsibility did God declare that it was not good for him to be alone and created Eve as a suitable helper (Genesis 2:18). This divine sequence emphasizes the importance of preparation, personal maturity, and alignment with God's purpose before entering marriage.

From the very beginning, God established the principles of purposeful labor and faithful stewardship. Adam's assignment in the garden afforded him the opportunity to develop a work ethic and to grow in his level of commitment. Adam's work was specific: to cultivate and guard what God had entrusted to him. In like manner, he would have the same assignment to guard his wife and help her grow into the woman God created her to be. Adam had to be diligent in his duties, as the success of the garden depended on his faithfulness, just as the success of his marriage would be dependent upon his faithfulness to his wife. Adam's management of the garden and his covenant with his wife would serve as the template of commitment for centuries to come.

Howbeit, today's societal norms and values often stand in stark opposition to the Word of God, evolving in ways that increasingly diverge from His design. The sanctity of marriage is frequently disregarded, divorce is viewed casually, premarital sex is normalized, and the belief that truth and morality are subjective and socially constructed has gained widespread acceptance.

Additionally, biblical family roles have eroded, reflecting a broader cultural shift away from accountability to the Almighty God. In light of these deviations, the principle of Adam's accountability and commitment to God before receiving Eve as a wife provides timeless wisdom for establishing a relationship with God before entering a covenant with a spouse.

Although Adam's relationship with God started well, his failure to remain accountable and committed disrupted the divine order, weakening his ability to spiritually cover and lead Eve. Adam's assignment to oversee and maintain the garden was given before Eve was even created, making him ultimately responsible for the outcome. Eve was deceived, but Adam was in open rebellion against God. Adam's failure became evident when he allowed the serpent to deceive Eve without stepping in to provide protection or guidance. This moment revealed a critical lapse in his spiritual duty. Instead of covering Eve with wisdom and obedience, Adam passively participated in the act of rebellion, forfeiting his God-given role as the leader and protector within the relationship. His disobedience not only fractured their unity but also distorted the divine order God had established for their partnership.

Adam's failure to cover Eve illustrates how accountability and commitment to God are foundational for fulfilling roles within marriage. By disregarding his divine responsibilities, Adam exposed both himself and Eve to consequences that disrupted their relationship with God and with one another. Today's couples need spiritual leadership in marriage, where both spouses, particularly husbands, are called to remain accountable to God to effectively guide, support, and nurture their partners. Eve's deception and Adam's rebellion serve as a cautionary example of how neglecting spiritual commitment and accountability (first to God, and secondly to one another) can lead to division, confusion, and brokenness in relationships.

For any couple desiring to endure in a challenging world, these Biblical principles remain deeply relevant. Too often, relationships are pursued prematurely, driven by societal pressure, emotional longing, or external expectations, rather than a clear sense of personal direction or readiness. God's design suggests that a man should first establish a fruitful and purposeful life before seeking a wife. Nevertheless, I must add, that being "gainfully employed" goes beyond merely having a job; but it's a reflection of emotional, spiritual, and financial stability, as well as a willingness to serve God's broader plan.

For men, this means cultivating a life of accountability to God, responsibility for what's entrusted to your care, vision for your future, and integrity in your dealings. For women, it is a reminder to seek a partner who is aligned with God's purpose, prepared to lead with accountability, and your own willingness to be a true helpmeet. The concept of being "fruitful before finding a wife" invites both men and women to approach relationships with intentionality and wisdom, creating marriages rooted in stability, shared purpose, and spiritual harmony. In a culture that often prioritizes instant gratification over lasting commitment, this biblical model offers a countercultural yet profoundly life-giving framework for building God-honoring unions.

The Commitment to Leave, Cleave, and Become One Flesh

Genesis 2:18 states, "And the Lord God said, it is not good that the man should be alone; I will make him a help meet for him." And in Genesis 2:24, the Lord provides instruction on how to care for this gift of woman that was bestowed upon him.

Genesis 2:24, "Therefore, shall a man leave his father and his mother, and shall cleave unto his wife: and they shall be one flesh." The instructions listed three directives to facilitate a God-honoring happy marriage 1) leave 2) cleave and 3) become one flesh.

- **TO LEAVE—To depart or move away from.**

To fully embrace the unity of marriage. One of the first, yet often most challenging steps is to "leave" your parents. The word used for "leave" in Genesis 2:24 goes beyond a simple parting—it conveys a deeper, more complete separation. In Greek, the word *kataleipo* intensifies the meaning, suggesting a decisive and intentional departure. This isn't merely a physical act but an emotional and relational shift that reorders priorities.

When a husband and wife leave their parents to commit to their marriage, they are establishing independence in every aspect of their life: emotionally, financially, spiritually, etc. Physical distance alone doesn't guarantee separation. You can live 3000 miles away and still be emotionally and financially dependent upon your parents as evident by maintaining phone calls for emotional support and borrowing money to assist with financial obligations (both signs of dependence).

Leaving your parents does not mean you cannot contact them or maintain a relationship with them. But it does require you to create some space from them in an effort to solidify your bond with your spouse so that your parents are no longer your first priority, but your husband or your wife is. This shift in priority has nothing to do with neglecting or dishonoring parents, but it's about prioritizing the new family unit. It's about building trust and unity in the marital relationship. When husbands and wives continue to seek emotional support from their parents, rather than their spouse, it may be a result of not giving the spouse the opportunity to fulfill that role.

When a man and woman marry, they enter a new, sacred union that supersedes all former relationships. Their bond must become the most important human relationship in their lives—more intimate, more loyal, and more enduring than any other.

In Genesis 12:1 the Lord tells Abram to leave his native country, his relatives, and his father's family and go to the land that the Lord would show him. As Abram and Sarai would become the father and mother of future generations to come, they would need to leave the systems and people that did not align with God's will for their lives. After Abram's and Sarai's successful departure from the Ur of the Chaldeans (their family), we begin to see them advancing in a more productive direction.

In Genesis 12:1, God calls Abram to a life-altering journey of faith, instructing him to leave behind his native country, his relatives, and his father's household to go to a land that He would show him. This command was not simply about geographic relocation but a profound spiritual transition that required Abram and Sarai to sever ties with systems, practices, and influences that were incompatible with God's divine purpose for their lives. The Ur of the Chaldeans, their homeland, was steeped in idolatry and traditions that would have hindered their ability to fully obey and trust God. By calling them out of this environment, God was setting them apart for a unique covenant relationship that would impact not only their own lives but also future generations.

Abram's obedience to this call was pivotal. Leaving behind the familiar required immense faith and trust, as God's command came with no specific destination initially revealed, only the promise of a land that He would show them. Sarai's participation in this journey demonstrated her own faith and commitment, as she willingly left the security of her home and family to follow her husband into the unknown.

For many couples today, this level of surrender is not an easy task. Family often serves as a foundation of support, comfort, and identity, shaping our values, decisions, and sense of belonging. The thought of stepping away from their influence, especially when it has been central to our lives, can feel overwhelming. Yet, just as Abram and Sarai trusted God and moved forward, couples who desire to thrive in God's design must also choose to prioritize His plan over familial or cultural expectations. True flourishing in marriage begins with obedience to His leading, even when it challenges deeply ingrained ties or traditions.

Abram and Sarai's departure from Ur marked the beginning of a transformation. Free from the distractions and influences of their former environment, they were positioned to hear God's voice more clearly and move in the direction He intended. As they traveled, God began to bless and prosper them, establishing Abram as the father of many nations and Sarai as the mother of future generations. This act of obedience laid the foundation for the covenant God would make with Abram, promising that through him all the families of the earth would be blessed (Genesis 12:2–3).

Abram and Sarai's journey reminds us that obedience to God's call often requires leaving behind not only physical places but also the systems, relationships, and mindsets that are contrary to His will. Their story demonstrates the importance of trusting God even when the path is unclear, and it highlights the spiritual growth and blessings that come from stepping out in faith. For modern believers, their example challenges us to examine what we might need to leave behind to fully embrace God's plans for our lives. It also affirms that when we prioritize God's call over worldly attachments, He leads us into a more productive and spiritually fulfilling direction, just as He did for Abram and Sarai.

- **TO CLEAVE-To join, to adhere firmly to, to cling to.**

To cleave means to stick, to be glued or bonded together. When a husband and wife come together in marriage, this joining is a ceremonial act—a legal agreement and a profound spiritual union created by God Himself. This bond is God's own "glue," stronger than any earthly adhesive, binding two souls together in a way that is designed to last a lifetime. It is a divine connection meant to endure, transcending time and circumstances, and reflecting God's intention for marriage as a lasting covenant.

To cleave to one another is to fully commit beyond the excitement of the wedding day and every day thereafter. It is a covenantal promise to be dependable, honest, faithful, and genuine. It is a vow to face every challenge together, as expressed in the marriage promise: "til death do us part," not until it becomes inconvenient or difficult. This commitment to cleave to your spouse is about enduring through all seasons, grounded in the choice to honor and love each other regardless of the circumstances.

Marriage is not something to be taken casually or entered into lightly. Jesus Himself declares in Matthew 19:6, "What God has joined together, let no man separate." Marriage, as God designed it, is meant to be a permanent covenant, only ended by death. Therefore, cleaving, staying committed to your spouse, is critical to the success of the marriage. A marriage can survive the loss of a child, infidelity, financial ruin, demanding parents, and even struggles with intimacy, but without the resolve to stick together through every trial, no marriage can truly thrive.

Cleaving means making a steadfast commitment to never give up. It signifies that divorce is not an option, even when life becomes challenging. Beloved, life will test you and your marriage in ways you may not expect. There will be moments when you question your commitment and feel tempted to walk away. However, to cleave means you're unwilling to leave! Cleaving means you choose to stay, no matter how heavy the trials may feel. It's a vow to endure together, trusting that perseverance will strengthen your bond and see you through the storms.

It is the same unwavering commitment that Jesus shows in our relationship with Him. Even when we are uncertain or struggling in our walk with Him, He remains steadfast, never abandoning us. Just as Jesus continues to be committed to us, offering love and grace when we falter or question our relationship with Him, a husband and wife are called to stay committed, regardless of circumstances. The faithfulness of our Lord serves as the ultimate model for our marriages, reminding us that true love and commitment are not dependent on how we feel in the moment, but on a deeper, unconditional devotion to each other, just as Christ remains devoted to us.

- **TO BECOME ONE FLESH-Developing sexual, spiritual, and emotional oneness. Becoming united with one's spouse.**

In Genesis 2:21–23, God created the woman from Adam's rib, signifying the complementary and equal nature of men and women in God's design for marriage. When God created Eve from Adam's rib, it was not from his head to rule over him, nor from his feet to be beneath him, but from his side to be beside him. This indicates that Eve was created as a partner, equal in worth and dignity, intended to walk alongside Adam in mutual support and shared responsibility.

The rib signifies protection and closeness. The rib is a vital part of the body, providing protection for the heart and lungs, symbolizing that Eve was to be a protector and nurturer of Adam's heart, and vice versa. It also highlights the idea of intimacy and unity, as the rib is deeply integrated into the structure of the body, signifying that the marital relationship is to be deeply intimate, emotionally and spiritually connected.

Additionally, the rib points to the idea of oneness and unity. As the two were originally one, taken from the same flesh, marriage restores this oneness, with the husband and wife becoming "one flesh" once again (Genesis 2:24, Ephesians 5:31). This deep unity reflects the relationship between Christ and the Church, as the Church is seen as the body of Christ, united with Him as His bride.

Ultimately, Eve being taken from Adam's rib speaks of the divine intention for marriage: mutual support, equality, intimacy, and the sacred union between husband and wife that reflects the unity of God's creation. It demonstrates God's purposeful design for man and woman to complement one another, building a foundation for both spiritual and relational harmony in marriage.

Commitment to Sexual Intimacy
Genesis 2:7–8, 15, 18–24.

7 And the Lord God formed man of the dust of the ground and breathed into his nostrils the breath of life; and man became a living soul.

8 And the Lord God planted a garden eastward in Eden; and there he put the man whom he had formed.

15 And the Lord God took the man, and put him into the garden of Eden to dress it and to keep it.

18 And the Lord god said, It is not good that the man should be alone; I will make him a help meet for him.

19 And out of the ground the Lord God formed every beast of the field, and every fowl of the air; and brought them unto Adam to see what he would call them: and whatsoever Adam called every living creature, that was the name thereof.

20 And Adam gave names to all cattle, and to the fowl of the air, and to every beast of the field; but for Adam there was not found a help meet for him.

21 And the Lord God caused a deep sleep to fall upon Adam, and he slept: and he took one of his ribs, and closed up the flesh instead thereof;

22 And the rib, which the Lord God had taken from man, made he a woman, and brought her unto the man.

23 And Adam said, This is now bone of my bones, and flesh of my flesh: she shall be called Woman, because she was taken out of Man.

24 Therefore shall a man leave his father and his mother and shall cleave unto his wife: and they shall be one flesh.

On a very fundamental level, the concept of "becoming one flesh" emphasizes a deep and sacred physical union. This principle reflects God's intention for marriage to be more than a legal or emotional bond. The physical act of sexual intimacy, which consummates the marriage, serves as the ultimate expression of unity, an intense act where two individuals become one in body. More than physical pleasure, marriage is sacrificial giving between a husband and wife.

Sex within marriage is a divine gift designed to strengthen the bond between husband and wife. When they come together in this intimate act, they physically embody the "one flesh" principle, where their bodies are united in a way that reflects their emotional and spiritual connection. The act of sex within marriage is inherently spiritual. It honors God's covenant for marriage, provides the potential for procreation, and symbolizes the offering of oneself to one's spouse, often as an act of sacrifice, especially when tired or facing challenges. Furthermore, it serves as a safeguard for the marriage, protecting it from external temptations such as pornography, infidelity, and sexual immorality.

Through sexual intimacy, a couple surrenders themselves to each other fully, giving up themselves without reservation or selfishness, and reflecting a deep spiritual commitment to one another.

The power of sex in marriage is significant because it involves mutual giving, allows the couple to experience a sense of belonging and closeness, fulfilling the purpose of the "one flesh" union that God created in the Garden of Eden. When sex is approached with love and respect, it becomes a means of bonding and reinforcing the emotional and spiritual connection between husband and wife.

Couples should make a concerted effort to kindle and deepen their sexual intimacy. When couples are not engaging in sex, the effects on the marriage can be profound, as this lack of intimacy can create distance and misunderstandings that weaken the marital bond. Sexual intimacy often serves as a means of expressing love, vulnerability, and trust, reinforcing the unique connection between husband and wife. Without it, emotional closeness is eroded, leaving the couple feeling disconnected, leading to feelings of loneliness, frustration, or rejection. Over time, this emotional gap can contribute to resentment or insecurity, as one or both partners may question their desirability or the health of the relationship.

Benefits of Sexual Intimacy

When couples engage in intercourse, an array of complex physiological processes take place that affect both partners in deeply interconnected ways. One of the most significant physiological responses during sex is the release of hormones. These hormones, particularly **oxytocin**, **dopamine**, and **endorphins**, play key roles in bonding, pleasure, and stress relief.

Oxytocin, often called the "love hormone," is released in large amounts during sex and especially during orgasm. It creates feelings of closeness and attachment, helping partners feel more emotionally connected. This hormone is also important in strengthening the bond between mother and child, which highlights its role in creating deep connections.

Dopamine, known as the "reward" hormone, is released during sexual activity and provides a sense of pleasure and satisfaction. It drives the feelings of joy and fulfillment associated with sexual connection. The release of dopamine provides a natural mood boost. These neurochemicals promote happiness and feelings of relaxation, which helps individuals feel less anxious and more content.

Endorphins, the body's natural painkillers, are released during sex, which help reduce pain and stress, leaving partners feeling more relaxed and euphoric. Many individuals report a decrease in pain, such as headaches, menstrual cramps, and even chronic pain conditions, following sexual activity due to the pain-relieving effects of these hormones.

One study conducted at Wilkes University in Pennsylvania found that couples who engage in sex once or twice a week have higher levels of immunoglobulin A (IgA), an antibody that defends against illness.

Sexual activity is also a form of physical exercise with numerous health benefits. During sexual intercourse, the body undergoes various physical responses that promote health and well-being. One of the most immediate effects is an increase in heart rate, which is similar to other forms of aerobic exercise. As the heart works harder to pump blood throughout the body, circulation is improved, which can help enhance overall cardiovascular health. This increase in blood flow also facilitates the delivery of oxygen and nutrients to various tissues, supporting organ function and improving energy levels.

Sexual activity also engages several muscle groups, particularly those in the pelvic region, core, and lower body. These muscles are often used in coordinated movements during intercourse, and regular activity can help strengthen them over time. Additionally, the physical exertion involved can improve flexibility and stamina.

Studies have shown that regular sexual activity may help lower the risk of heart disease and improve overall heart function by stimulating circulation and helping maintain healthy blood pressure levels. In particular, the cardiovascular benefits associated with sexual activity resemble those of moderate physical exercise. For example, regular sexual activity has been linked to improved cholesterol levels and a decreased risk of developing hypertension.

In addition, the positive physical effects of sex extend beyond just cardiovascular benefits. It can also help promote better sleep by releasing oxytocin and prolactin, hormones that induce relaxation and feelings of contentment. The act of sexual intimacy can contribute to overall physical fitness by engaging muscles and increasing blood flow, further supporting the body's natural healing and regeneration processes.

Scriptural References for Sexual Intimacy
Proverbs 5:18–20 (NLT)

18 Let your wife be a fountain of blessing for you. Rejoice in the wife of your youth.

19 She is a loving deer, a graceful doe. Let her breasts satisfy you always. May you always be captivated by her love.

20 Why be captivated, my son, by an immoral woman, or fondle the breasts of a promiscuous woman?

Song of Songs 3:1–4 (NLT)

1 One night as I lay in bed, I yearned for my lover. I yearned for him, but he did not come.

2 So I said to myself, "I will get up and roam the city, searching in the streets and squares. I will search for the one I love." So I searched everywhere but did not find him.

3 The watchmen stopped me as they made their rounds, and I asked, "Have you seen the one I love?"

4 Then scarcely had I left them when I found my love! I caught and held him tightly, then I brought him to my mother's house, into my mother's bed, where I had been conceived.

Hebrews 13:4 (NLT)

4 Give honor to marriage and remain faithful to one another in marriage. God will surely judge people who are immoral and those who commit adultery.

1 Corinthians 7:3–5 (NLT)

3 The husband should fulfill his wife's sexual needs, and the wife should fulfill her husband's needs.

4 The wife gives authority over her body to her husband, and the husband gives authority over his body to his wife.

5 Do not deprive each other of sexual relations, unless you both agree to refrain from sexual intimacy for a limited time so you can give yourselves more completely to prayer. Afterward, you should come together again so that Satan won't be able to tempt you because of your lack of self-control.

Benefits of Emotional Intimacy

In the context of marriage, becoming "one flesh" signifies much more than sexual intimacy. While the physical act of union is an important expression of marital love, the deeper meaning lies in the sacredness of that union, which extends to emotional and spiritual dimensions as well. The idea of becoming one flesh is about the holistic connection between spouses, an intertwining of hearts, minds, and souls. Emotional intimacy is an ongoing process of merging lives, priorities, and identities in a way that creates an inseparable bond. This emotional bond, rooted in deep love and commitment is designed to be exclusive to the relationship between husband and wife, making their connection unique and sacred.

Emotional intimacy plays a pivotal role in nurturing the oneness between partners. It involves sharing the good, the bad, and the ugly; the raw and vulnerable parts of oneself. It's sharing the fears, insecurities, hopes, and dreams that one might otherwise not share with anyone else. In a marriage, emotional intimacy is what allows each spouse to see the other as they truly are, without the masks that might be worn in other areas of life. This level of openness cultivates trust and mutual understanding. As both partners become more open and transparent, they create a safe space in the marriage where both can feel secure enough to express their innermost thoughts and feelings. In turn, this trust deepens their bond and increases their capacity to support each other, even through difficult times.

The beauty of emotional intimacy lies in how couples become deeply attuned to each other's needs, responding with empathy, understanding, and genuine care. The more emotionally connected spouses are, the better they are at anticipating each other's emotional states and providing the support needed. This kind of connection transcends physical intimacy; it builds a foundation of trust and support that can weather the ups and downs of life. Spouses who prioritize emotional intimacy are more likely to engage in meaningful conversations, resolve conflicts constructively, and create a partnership that is grounded in a deep understanding of each other.

When spouses are emotionally in tune, they become more effective partners in every aspect of life—whether it's raising children, managing finances, or simply enjoying life's small moments together. The emotional connection deepens their love and commitment, creating a bond that is not easily broken.

Benefits of Spiritual Intimacy

Becoming one flesh also manifests itself in spiritual intimacy. Spiritual intimacy, while often overlooked or not fully explored, is an essential and transformative aspect of marital oneness. At its core, spiritual intimacy in marriage is grounded in a shared faith, shared values, and a shared commitment to God. This intimacy is cultivated when both spouses align their lives with divine purpose, not only as individuals but as a couple united in their spiritual journey. When couples pray together, study Scripture, or worship as one, they intentionally invite God into their union. This act of inviting God's presence into the union is incredibly powerful because it infuses the marriage with a divine strength, protection, and guidance that goes far beyond human understanding.

Many couples may not recognize the profound impact that spiritual intimacy can have on their relationship. In a world that often prioritizes sexual connection or emotional closeness, the idea of deepening spiritual intimacy may seem abstract or secondary. However, when two individuals are committed to growing in faith together, they build a partnership that is rooted in something far greater than their own efforts. Spiritual intimacy yields unity in a unique way. It aligns the couple's hearts and minds toward God's will for their lives, reinforcing the covenant of marriage with a divine purpose. This unity is not limited to a fleeting emotional or physical connection but is sustained by the eternal bond of their shared faith. When couples face challenges, having this spiritual connection creates a foundation that helps them endure trials with a sense of peace and assurance, knowing that God is at the center of their relationship.

Moreover, spiritual intimacy includes living out one's faith together in everyday life—how the husband treats his wife and how the wife treats her husband in the small moments when no one is watching. Spiritual intimacy is developed in the way they support each other in their spiritual growth, and how they model their beliefs to each other and to those around them. A spiritually intimate marriage calls for an ongoing commitment to grow together in faith, particularly when life presents challenges.

Apostle and I have faced some incredibly tough seasons in our marriage, and it was only by the grace of God that we made it through. The trials we encountered early on taught us to lean into God and trust Him completely, developing our spiritual intimacy in ways we never expected. When you're unsure of what to do or where to turn, you learn to rely on prayer and faith, trusting that God will guide you through.

As we matured, the challenges we faced only strengthened our spiritual bond. We chose not to fix our eyes on external solutions or the people around us, but we trusted the Lord, knowing that He would work everything together for our good. This brought us closer than ever. We stopped viewing challenges as insurmountable obstacles and began to see them as opportunities to draw nearer to God and to each other. With every trial, our faith grew stronger, and so did our connection. We saw how God used our struggle as stepping stones to create deeper unity, reminding us that when we stand together in faith, anchored in God, there's nothing we cannot overcome.

Being one flesh in marriage is a divine covenant that encompasses the fullness of a couple's connection: sexually/physically, emotionally, and spiritually. It's a commitment that invites both partners to engage in a shared journey of growth, intimacy, and mutual respect. Physically, it's an expression of love and unity, but holistically, all three (including emotional and spiritual dimensions also) contribute to a profound sacred bond. They work synergistically to create the best marital union possible.

A marriage that thrives in oneness is one where each partner actively nurtures the other's well-being in every aspect of life. It's through this holistic connection where love, support, faith, and commitment intersect that couples reflect the beauty of God's design, becoming a testament and reflection of His love and grace. This profound oneness is a dynamic, ongoing journey that strengthens with each shared experience, challenge, and triumph, drawing the couple ever closer to each other and to the heart of God.

Chapter Reflections

Marriage is a covenant that demands unwavering commitment, not just on the wedding day but throughout the lifetime journey of two individuals becoming one. This commitment is multifaceted, involving the decision to leave one's family of origin, cleave to one's spouse, and become one flesh. These foundational principles set the tone for a marriage rooted in loyalty, sacrifice, and unity, and they call for deliberate, ongoing efforts to nurture and protect the bond.

The act of "leaving" signifies a purposeful separation from a person's family of origin to establish a new family unit with their spouse. This is not about severing relationships but rather about reprioritizing them. The primary loyalty must shift to the spouse, creating a strong and exclusive partnership. The concept of "cleaving" represents the intentional and enduring bond between husband and wife, marked by steadfast commitment and mutual devotion. Becoming "one flesh" encapsulates the holistic unity of marriage, a unity that spans physical, emotional, and spiritual dimensions. This divine design for marriage reflects God's intention for a resilient and sacred union, requiring couples to invest time, effort, and love to grow together.

Sexual intimacy is a vital expression of this "one flesh" principle. It goes beyond physical pleasure, serving as a powerful symbol of the love and commitment shared between husband and wife. The Bible stresses its significance in passages like 1 Corinthians 7:3–5, encouraging spouses to prioritize this connection and not deprive one another. Regular sexual intimacy lends to trust, reduces stress, and strengthens both the emotional and physical connection within the marriage. It also acts as a safeguard against external temptations, reinforcing the exclusivity and sanctity of the marital bond.

Beyond the physical, intimacy in marriage also involves emotional and spiritual connection. Emotional intimacy is the bedrock of trust and transparency, creating a safe space where spouses can share their thoughts, feelings, and vulnerabilities. Spouses need to be assured that their partners get them. This deepens their understanding of one another and builds a sense of security and partnership. Simultaneously, spiritual intimacy is foundational to a thriving marriage. When couples pray together, study Scripture, and worship as one, they align their relationship with God's will. This spiritual bond invites God's presence into their union, providing guidance and strength to navigate life's challenges.

The benefits of these forms of intimacy are profound. Sexual intimacy promotes unity and mutual affection, enhancing overall marital satisfaction. Emotional intimacy builds closeness and trust, fostering a partnership that can withstand life's ups and downs. Spiritual intimacy anchors the marriage in God's purpose, offering clarity and resilience when trials arise. Together, these aspects of intimacy create a marriage that is fulfilling, enduring, and reflective of God's design.

In conclusion, commitment in marriage is an ongoing choice, a decision to leave, cleave, and embrace the oneness that marriage entails. By nurturing intimacy on all levels and prioritizing their relationship, couples can experience a union marked by love, unity, and joy. This commitment, rooted in God's plan, transforms marriage into a sacred and enduring partnership, bringing glory to Him and deep fulfillment to the spouses.

Prayer

Dear Lord,

Help us to live as one flesh, unified in mind, body, and spirit so that our marriage glorifies You. May our thoughts, actions, and decisions reflect a commitment to working together, serving one another selflessly, and prioritizing our union above all else except our relationship with You.

Teach us, Lord, to truly leave behind anything, past relationships, selfish ambitions, or unhealthy ties, that hinders our ability to fully embrace this union. May we cling to each other with unwavering loyalty, finding joy and strength in the bond You have ordained.

Father, empower us to cleave to one another, not just in physical closeness but in emotional intimacy, spiritual unity, and shared purpose. Let no outside force or worldly distraction separate what You have joined together. Teach us to support, honor, and uplift each other in love, even in the face of challenges.

In Jesus' Name, we pray, Amen.

CHAPTER 3

Healthy Harmonious Home:
Marital Roles and Responsibilities

"Your wife will be like a fruitful vine within your house, your children will be like olive shoots around your table. Yes, this will be the blessing for the man who fears the Lord."

(Psalm 128:3–4)

Imagine marriage as a beautifully orchestrated duet, where each note and harmony has been thoughtfully designed, not to overshadow one another but to create a masterpiece together. In such a composition, each partner's unique strengths and rhythms blend seamlessly, creating a relationship that reflects beauty, unity, and purpose. Like any great work of art, this harmony is not accidental, it is the result of intentional effort, mutual respect, and a shared commitment to the greater good of the whole. When both partners embrace their distinct roles, their combined melody becomes more powerful and profound than either could produce alone.

This type of divine configuration contrasts sharply with the dissonance that often characterizes modern relationships, weighed down by misunderstandings or struggles for equality, power, and control. Yet, the Bible offers a more profound vision for marriage. It describes the roles and responsibilities of husbands and wives not as competing melodies but as two parts of a unified whole, intricately woven together to reflect something greater than themselves: God's relationship with the Church.

Marital roles and responsibilities aren't about who's stronger or more important; they're about complementing each other's strengths, balancing each other's needs, and serving each other with love and purpose. When two people embrace this design, they discover a harmony that reaches beyond the everyday and taps into something divine. This doesn't come easily—it requires humility, grace, and selflessness, but the result is a partnership that delivers joy and glorifies God.

When we look at the roles within marriage, it's essential to see them through a lens of deep commitment and humble service to one another—roles not meant to impose limits but to reveal the true strength that comes from mutual support. Marriage, as God designed it, is far from the romanticized ideal many envision. Instead, it's a calling that asks each partner to serve selflessly, honoring the unique gifts and callings of the other. What if the true fulfillment in marriage doesn't lie in determining who's "in charge" but rather in embracing each other's strengths as a means to grow together? This journey toward a God-centered marriage is one that reflects His covenant love and grace: a path that, when wholeheartedly embraced, has the power to transform the marriage itself and to inspire others who witness such genuine devotion.

The Husband's Leadership

In Scripture, husbands and fathers are given the weighty responsibility of leading their homes. This leadership, however, is rooted in love, humility, and service, not dominance or control. The Bible portrays leadership in the home as a sacrificial role where the man is called to model Christ-like love, servant leadership, and wisdom. Yet, the challenges that come with this role are numerous, often demanding spiritual maturity, emotional intelligence, and resilience.

Husbands are called to be the spiritual leaders of their households. In 1 Corinthians 11:3, Paul declares, "But I want you to understand that the head of every man is Christ, the head of a wife is her husband, and the head of Christ is God." This headship is meant to reflect Christ's selflessness, sacrifice, and humility, demonstrating servant leadership. A husband's leadership is therefore an act of servitude, emulating Christ's selfless love that sacrifices for the well-being of the beloved. This requires him to make decisions with his family's best interests at heart, to guide them in spiritual matters, and to model a godly example in his own actions and character.

In a biblical marriage, the roles of husband and wife are rooted in God's design for a loving and balanced partnership. Ephesians 5:25–28 offers a profound model for the husband's role, describing how he is to love his wife "as Christ loved the church and gave himself up for her." This sacrificial love is the foundation of his role as a leader. Far from implying dominance, this role speaks to a form of leadership rooted in humility, protection, and service.

This Christ-like love calls the husband to a standard that challenges him to go beyond the superficial; he is to lead with gentleness, wisdom, and integrity, always seeking the best for his wife. His leadership is characterized by active support, emotional security, and spiritual guidance, creating an environment where his wife feels protected, cherished, and encouraged to flourish. When a husband embraces his role in this way, he embodies God's grace, leading through nurturing love that invites his wife into a place of safety and trust. This type of leadership sets the stage for a godly marriage, one where both husband and wife are able to fulfill their roles in harmony with each other and in obedience to God's purpose.

In my own marriage of 35 years, it has been so comforting to have my husband to lead our family through his Christian devotion. Let me be the first to tell you, "It hasn't always been that way!" In our earlier years of marriage when we were teenagers, we did not have a complete understanding of the roles and responsibilities of a husband and wife. We came from different family upbringings, and it was a challenge to find common ground. Consequently, we fought often out of a selfish will to have our own way despite God's design for us.

Then we finally had an epiphany! We both loved the Lord (check). We both declared to be Christians (check). We both agreed that the Bible was our guide wherein we patterned our lives after (check). We said the word of God was our final authority (check). Well since we agreed on all this, there was no reason to disagree with one another when the word of God was our guide, our instruction manual for governing our daily affairs—it was our substrata.

As I matured in my walk with Christ, it was difficult to oppose my husband's leadership when I knew his direction was coming from the Word of God. Those moments when I chose not to honor his spiritual leadership, revealed one of two things about me: Either I did not believe the word of God myself or I was being a hypocrite! Hearing and agreeing to the teachings of the word, but not adjusting my actions to do them. James 1:22 declares, "But don't just listen to God's word. You must do what it says. Otherwise, you are only fooling yourselves."

Biblical Foundations of Leadership

The Bible offers us a picture of what it means to be a husband and father, particularly in passages like Ephesians 5:22–33 and 1 Peter 3:7 (treating the wife with understanding). In Ephesians 5:25, Paul instructs husbands, "Love your wives, just as Christ loved the church and gave himself up for her." This kind of leadership is sacrificial and others-focused, reflecting how Christ leads His people by laying down His life. The husband, in turn, is called to guide and protect his family, making decisions that align with God's will and are beneficial to the spiritual and physical well-being of his wife and children.

In Ephesians 6:4, fathers are also tasked with nurturing their children, instructing them in the ways of the Lord: "Fathers, do not provoke your children to anger, but bring them up in the discipline and instruction of the Lord." Here, leadership extends beyond providing material needs; it includes the spiritual formation and character development of their children, modeling integrity, discipline, and compassion. One of the greatest gifts a father can provide for his children is the gift of his constant presence where his devotion is spent on their development and wellbeing.

Traditionally, the role of a husband and father has been defined by the expectation to provide financially for his wife and children. However, God's standard calls for far more. For too long, being a "good father" was measured solely by hard work and financial provision. While these are important, they fall short of what is truly needed. Families face countless challenges every day, and a father's active presence is not just desired but essential. To nurture and raise healthy, well-rounded children, a father must be fully engaged—emotionally, spiritually, and physically—offering guidance, love, and support in addition to material provision.

Fatherhood leadership involves being fully present and intentionally nurturing the overall well-being of the family. Husbands may not always provide the right answers for every situation, but they should be committed to finding the necessary solutions to safeguard their family's welfare as this defines true leadership. A good father understands that leadership isn't perfection, but ongoing progress. However, leading a family isn't a solo mission; it's a partnership with one's spouse as each partner is learning and growing with the family. As husbands and wives acclimate to their roles in their nuclear family, there will be mistakes. The Bible serves as the believer's instruction manual, but it will often require time and patience to execute the responsibilities accordingly.

For the family to experience its greatest success, husbands should view their wives as equally invested partners in making decisions that shape the family's future as it impacts the stability of the entire household. This shared responsibility should be modeled before your children because it reflects balance and teamwork. Your children are watching your actions and observing how their parents are doing family life. Today's youth see past the old adage of "Do as I say, not as I do." Instead, they look to their parents' actions to see if they align with what they say. Living out what is taught is essential for parents who want to model Christ-like behavior and show that this way of life is genuinely attainable. Without this consistency, kids often see their parents as hypocritical, and their advice loses influence and impact.

As fathers cover and partner with their wives in leading their families, they play an important role in encouraging a balanced home with balanced activities. Fathers can take the initiative by promoting family time that involves shared experiences, such as outdoor adventures, game nights, or even regular meals together. These moments strengthen family bonds and create a sense of belonging and emotional security, which are vital for every family member's mental well-being.

Equally important is setting limits on technology use. In today's digital age, screens dominate much of our time, often leading to decreased physical activity, disrupted sleep, and reduced face-to-face interactions. Fathers, as leaders, can model healthy technology habits by setting limits on their own phone use, creating designated tech-free zones during meals, and limiting screen time before bed. By doing so, they encourage their children to engage in more meaningful activities like reading, hobbies, or simply spending time outdoors. These activities not only nurture the body and mind but also teach valuable life skills like teamwork, perseverance, and self-expression, keeping everyone's mental and physical health in check.

When my husband and I were raising our children during their grade school years, we set clear boundaries around technology to prioritize family connections and create meaningful interactions. Televisions were not allowed in their bedrooms, and they were not permitted to keep phones in their possession overnight. At dinner, electronic devices such as phones, tablets, or gaming consoles were strictly off-limits. This created an atmosphere where conversation could flourish, and it allowed us to fully engage with one another.

We made it a priority to genuinely inquire about their day, not the casual, surface-level "How was your day?" that often leads to a quick "Fine" before moving on. Instead, we engaged in intentional check-ins, opening a space where they felt heard and valued. We offered our full, undivided attention, listening thoughtfully to their experiences, challenges, and triumphs. In return, we expected the same level of attentiveness from them, which led to meaningful conversations that deepened our connection as a family.

These intentional practices became a cornerstone of our family dynamic. Now as adults, our children often reflect on their upbringing, attributing much of their success and emotional well-being to the consistency of a dual-parent household where both parents were actively involved in their development and shared in the richness of the family experience.

When considering finances, leading means thinking ahead, making sacrifices when needed, and being intentional with resources. Much like Adam, fathers must attend to their "gardens." He must work the land by earning financial means to support his family (Genesis 2:15), and he has to watch over it by wisely managing what he has earned. This principle sets a tone for responsibility, teaching his kids the value of hard work and delayed gratification.

Money can be a sensitive topic, but when a father shares the "why" behind financial choices, he teaches his family biblical stewardship, builds trust, and sets a powerful example of faith and patience. When it came to finances, my husband and I would explain to our children why we were making certain financial decisions and why one family goal took priority over impulse spending. We gave them counsel on honoring God in their finances, ways to save as a family for something meaningful, and the detriments of being wasteful. By handling finances with a forward-thinking mindset, fathers can teach their children that wise stewardship is about balance, using what you have today in a way that benefits tomorrow.

Overall, the husband/father role is more impactful if he lives daily in a way that makes faith real and visible. He's called to be an example of what it means to live with integrity, kindness, and faith. This might look like prioritizing prayer, being honest about challenges, or making time to discuss the things that affect their life.

It is often in the small, consistent actions that a man can encourage his family's spiritual growth. Praying together and listening to each other's concerns models grace in both good and difficult times. By cultivating a home where faith is as much practiced openly as it is talked about, fathers can create a space where their family feels safe to explore and strengthen their own beliefs.

I am always encouraged when I hear children honor their parents as heroes and role models, which I believe reflects the powerful effects of authentic, Christ-centered parenting. For husbands, leading in this way takes humility, patience, and a commitment to growing alongside their family.

Embracing this role means learning as he goes, being open to change, and continuously striving to reflect the values he hopes to pass on to his children. Mistakes and setbacks will happen, but when fathers lead with humility and dedication, they give their families a lasting example of what it means to live with purpose, care, and active faith.

Challenges in Leading a Modern Household

While the Bible outlines a clear role for husbands and fathers as leaders within the family, men today face unique challenges in fulfilling this calling. One of the biggest obstacles is the cultural shift toward egalitarian models of family, which often promote an equal sharing of roles but can lead to confusion about what healthy leadership looks like within a biblical framework. Many men struggle with understanding how to lead in a way that honors God without undermining the mutual respect and partnership they value with their wives. In a society that increasingly questions or even rejects traditional models of family roles, husbands may feel uncertain about how to balance their biblical calling to lead with a collaborative approach that respects their wife's equal voice and influence.

This confusion is often compounded by societal pressures that tend to de-emphasize, or even discourage the father's leadership role. In a culture that sometimes views male authority in the home as outdated or domineering, men can feel torn between following these evolving expectations and staying true to the biblical mandate to lead their families with wisdom, humility, and strength. The pressure to conform to societal norms, especially those that emphasize self-fulfillment and independence, may also lead some men to shy away from their roles as spiritual heads of their households. This tension can leave men feeling ill-equipped, and they may find themselves questioning what leadership should look like in a family that's both rooted in Scripture and in touch with today's realities.

At the heart of this struggle is the challenge of redefining leadership as service. The Bible's picture of a husband's role isn't about authority in a controlling sense but rather about selfless service and guidance, as Christ serves the Church. The husband's leadership should be a source of stability, emotional and spiritual support, and a consistent example of his faith. Many men today are finding that true leadership involves building up their wives and children through empathy, listening, and shared decision-making while still embracing the responsibility to provide spiritual direction and maintain a sense of purpose for their families. It's about leading with both strength and gentleness, grounded in love and a commitment to each family member's growth.

Despite these cultural pressures, many men are finding ways to lead authentically by embracing the biblical model of servant leadership. They're discovering that they can honor both their role as spiritual heads of the family and their respect for their wife's voice, strengths, and influence. This approach fosters a healthy dynamic in which both spouses work together to model Christ's love for their children, creating an environment where leadership isn't domineering which allows everyone to feel valued, supported, and spiritually nourished.

Another significant challenge is the demand for emotional depth. By emotional depth, I mean the ability to understand, express, and navigate one's emotions and the emotions of others with insight and authenticity. It involves being self-aware, empathetic, and capable of forming meaningful, intimate connections. Christian husbands and fathers are mindful that spiritual guidance is required to cultivate a Christ-centered family, but they may be hard-pressed to provide emotional stability. When men lack emotional awareness, it can hinder the closeness and openness that are vital to a strong marriage. A man who has not learned to process his emotions or is still growing in spiritual maturity may find it difficult to lead his family with the wisdom, grace, and empathy the role demands.

Without the proper tools to address emotions or a solid spiritual foundation to lean on, men will experience great opposition in creating and sustaining a sacred union in an ungodly world. Emotional struggles can manifest as an inability to communicate effectively, manage stress, or empathize with their spouse and children, leading to friction and a sense of disconnection within the family. A lack of vulnerability and self-awareness may also cause men to retreat, isolate, or respond in ways that feel cold or unapproachable to their loved ones. This makes it all the more vital for husbands and fathers to prioritize their own spiritual growth and emotional development, ensuring they can lead their families with strength, compassion, and resilience, grounded firmly in Christ.

To add to the list of challenges is the balance of work and family life. The dominant discourse often equates success with career accomplishments, financial status, and external achievements. This societal narrative can generate intense pressure to prioritize work over family. This perspective often results in emotional and spiritual absenteeism, where men may be physically present, but not truly engaged with their family's needs. Unfortunately, when the demands of work, personal achievements, and financial strains aren't properly balanced, they will drain energy and focus, hindering meaningful connections with spouses and children.

I have counseled many families grappling with this very issue. Fathers often work tirelessly to provide financial stability for their families, believing that their hard work and dedication are the ultimate expressions of love and care. In their minds, they are doing their best, offering what they feel their family needs most. Yet, despite their good intentions, they are often emotionally checked out, unaware of the struggles, needs, or even day-to-day experiences of their wife and children. This disconnect can lead to feelings of neglect within the family, causing resentment, misunderstanding, and a breakdown in communication.

The breakthrough for these families came when we worked together to create a healthier balance—one where career success remained a priority, but not at the expense of the family's emotional and spiritual well-being. By helping these fathers recognize the importance of being present and engaged, we were able to redefine success to include professional achievements and relational and spiritual growth at home.

We focused on practical steps, such as setting boundaries around work hours, intentionally carving out time for meaningful interactions with their family, and learning how to listen and connect on a deeper level. For some, this involved a shift in mindset, understanding that their presence and involvement at home are just as valuable as their financial contributions. For others, it required developing new habits, such as regular family check-ins, shared activities, or prioritizing one-on-one time with their spouse and children.

Ultimately, these changes transformed their relationships and brought a greater sense of fulfillment and purpose to their lives. As these fathers became more intentional about engaging with their families, they realized that a thriving home life is not a trade-off for career success but a vital component of their legacy. They began to see their roles as husbands and fathers not as competing with their professional ambitions but as complementary to them, with each area enriching the other.

By repositioning their priorities within God's design for family, they found a new rhythm that allowed them to lead with wisdom and balance. They learned to integrate their faith into both their work and home life and experienced success in both arenas. This shift not only strengthened the bonds within their families but also gave them a renewed perspective on what it truly means to succeed in every aspect of their lives.

Examples of Biblical Leadership and Its Challenges

1. *Abram*: In Genesis 16, we see Abram struggling to lead his household faithfully when his wife Sarai suggests that he have a child with Hagar. Abram's decision to go along with Sarai's suggestion, rather than waiting on God's promise, caused tension and division in the family.

2. *David*: Another example is David, who was a man after God's own heart but struggled with family leadership. His failure to confront

the sins within his household, such as with his son Amnon and daughter Tamar in 2 Samuel 13, shows the consequences of passive fatherhood. David's avoidance of conflict allowed bitterness and dysfunction to fester within his family.

3. _**Eli**_: In 1 Samuel 2–4, Eli, the high priest, was a well-intentioned leader but a largely ineffective father. His sons, Hophni and Phinehas, served as priests but were corrupt, exploiting their position for personal gain and disobeying God's laws. Despite knowing of their wrongdoing, Eli failed to discipline them adequately. His lack of corrective action led to their downfall and brought judgment upon his entire household.

4. _**Lot**_: In Genesis 19, Lot made several choices that jeopardized his family's well-being, including moving his family to Sodom, a city known for its immorality. He struggled to protect his family from the corrupt influences around them, leading to devastating consequences. His daughters, shaped by the environment they grew up in, ultimately made morally questionable decisions, resulting in further tragedy.

5. _**Jacob**_: While Jacob was a devoted father in some ways, his blatant favoritism toward his son Joseph caused severe division and resentment among his other sons (Genesis 37). By openly favoring Joseph, Jacob fostered jealousy, leading the brothers to sell Joseph into slavery. His lack of fairness and wisdom in parenting created family strife that could have been avoided with a more balanced guidance.

6. _**Samuel**_: Although Samuel was a strong spiritual leader for Israel, his own family life suffered (1 Samuel 8). His sons, Joel and Abijah, whom he appointed as judges, were corrupt and did not follow his example. The people of Israel eventually demanded a king because Samuel's sons were unfit to lead. Samuel's failure to hold his sons accountable impacted the nation as a whole.

7. _**Manasseh**_: In 2 Kings 21, Manasseh, one of the kings of Judah, set an extremely poor example for his children and the nation by leading them into idolatry and evil practices. He introduced pagan worship and even sacrificed one of his own sons, contributing to a cycle of corruption and turning away from God. His leadership negatively affected his family and all of Judah, demonstrating how a lack of godly guidance can have generational impacts.

These fathers and their stories serve as cautionary examples of how poor leadership and lack of accountability can affect families and even nations. Rather than seeing leadership solely in terms of decision-making authority and financial provision, husband/father leaders must realize that leadership also involves serving his family, being intentional about family connections, creating a loving environment, being emotionally available, and guiding the family toward a deeper relationship with God.

While the role of husband and father as the leader in the home is challenging, it is also a high calling filled with purpose and divine blessing. By seeking God's wisdom, embracing servant leadership, and being attentive to the emotional and spiritual needs of their families, men can lead their households in a way that reflects Christ's love for the church. Though cultural pressures and personal limitations may make this difficult, men are called to rise above these challenges with God's help, knowing that their efforts in leading their families will have an eternal impact.

Servant Leadership as the Model

The key to overcoming these challenges lies in understanding that biblical leadership is fundamentally servant leadership. Jesus said in Matthew 20:26–28, "Whoever wants to become great among you must be your servant . . . just as the Son of Man did not come to be served, but to serve." For husbands and fathers, this means putting the needs of their family above their own, nurturing their children's spiritual growth, and loving their wives sacrificially.

Leadership in the home is not a passive role but an active and intentional pursuit of godliness and service. It means leading by example—being the first to pray, the first to apologize, and the first to forgive. It also means engaging in conversations about faith, modeling humility, and encouraging open communication about struggles and victories alike.

The Husband's Love

With the Bible being the greatest book ever written, especially in the category of love, there is much to consider in this section. When it comes to love, husbands are called to love their wives with the same sacrificial and unconditional love that Christ shows to humanity. This concept is beautifully outlined in Ephesians 5, where we explore how husbands are to love their wives as Christ loved the church. Similarly, the Apostle Paul reiterates this principle in Colossians 3:19, where he admonishes, *"Husbands, love your wives and do not be harsh with them."* emphasizing gentleness, patience, and care in a husband's love toward his wife.

When the pressures of life weigh on us, we can become irritable, impatient, and intolerant of people including our spouses. It's hard to admit to this, but most of us are guilty of it; the sooner we recognize it, the quicker we're able to conquer it and move forward. When our partners are expressing their concerns and we feel challenged or confronted by their expressions, it is not uncommon to become snappy and moody in our disposition. So, the Apostle Paul admonishes husbands in their roles as leaders to take their leadership a step further and avoid being bitter and harsh toward their wives when such situations arise. The husband is admonished to love (to entreat gently) his wife in the same manner the Lord would deal with us. This love isn't based on convenience or self-interest but is marked by putting the wife's needs and well-being first. It requires patience, kindness, and a deep commitment to nurturing both her spiritual and emotional health.

This Christian love is very descriptive and is also outlined in 1 Corinthians 13:4–7. The Bible states that love is patient and kind—not envious, boastful, or arrogant. It's the kind of love that doesn't insist on its own way, and it's not easily angered or resentful.

Love is patient means a willingness to endure hardship and delay without frustration, while kindness involves showing genuine care, compassion, and thoughtfulness in our actions and words.

Love is not envious, meaning it does not covet or resent the success or possessions of others. It is also not boastful or arrogant, refraining from prideful self-promotion or treating others as inferior. Instead, love promotes humility, valuing others above oneself.

Love doesn't insist on its own way, highlighting the importance of compromise, selflessness, and mutual respect in relationships.

Love is also not easily angered or resentful, meaning it does not hold grudges or react impulsively to every disagreement. Instead, it breeds a spirit of forgiveness, allowing for healing and reconciliation.

If husbands and wives really took the time to examine these qualities and truly understand the implications of what's being stated, it could profoundly change how we approach marriage. Many marital conflicts arise from selfishness, impatience, pride, or a failure to communicate effectively. But if couples were to genuinely embrace the principles of love outlined in this passage, they would likely experience fewer misunderstandings, more compassion, greater harmony in their relationships, and significantly fewer divorces.

In practice, this love may find expression in a husband actively listening to his wife's concerns. Listening with the intent to understand versus trying to be understood. This love looks like a husband providing his wife with emotional support when she's feeling overwhelmed. It can include a husband taking the time to pray for his wife's spiritual growth and offering encouragement when she's struggling with her faith. This love can also be displayed by giving up personal comforts to make sure that his wife feels valued and cared for or making time to help her with daily responsibilities, showing her that she is a priority.

My husband and I view our marriage as a true partnership. We make it a priority not to let either of us become overwhelmed with any task or responsibility. For instance, if my husband is barbecuing, I'm in the kitchen preparing the side dishes, desserts, or cleaning up. When I handle the laundry, he helps with folding or putting it away. I'm never left alone to tackle a household chore while he relaxes, and vice versa. We both actively share in the work, as it's our way of showing love and appreciation for each other, ensuring that neither of us feels taken for granted.

One of the greatest acts of love that I experienced in my marriage was my husband's support of my ministry. Prior to my marriage, my pastor would occasionally ask me to speak at church programs during my teenage years. I tried to decline the request. I tried to hide. I made excuses. You name it, I endeavored to avoid ministering at all costs. I just wasn't ready to acknowledge a calling in my life. But after my husband and I married, he immediately stepped in where my pastor left off, encouraging and supporting me to embrace the calling I had been avoiding.

In the '90s, while there were certainly women preachers, it wasn't yet widely accepted for women to minister. Despite this, my husband recognized God's calling and anointing on my life and began assigning me preaching engagements at the church we pastored. When I felt uncertain or hesitant about the task, he would encourage me, reminding me that the Holy Spirit's presence and guidance would be with me if I simply submitted to His authority. When I reflect on my husband's role as a covering for me and my children, I recognize how palpable his love is for us.

A husband's love is demonstrated in his leadership, and it serves as a profound and intimate source of support and nurturing. I believe my husband's display of love reflects his respect for my unique gifts, dreams, and God-given purpose. He makes it obvious in the ways he actively seeks to help me grow, always encouraging me to flourish in the areas where God is calling me to step into my full potential. This kind of love values my individuality and aspirations, recognizing that my growth does not threaten his, but rather strengthens our partnership.

By supporting my calling, my husband acknowledged that I had my own identity and purpose beyond our marriage. Proverbs 31:10–31 celebrates a woman who is industrious, wise, and active in various spheres, from managing her household to conducting business and serving her community. A husband who encourages his wife in her pursuits shows that he values her as a partner, seeing her potential and contributions not only within the family but also in a broader capacity. This affirms her worth and dignity as an individual created in the image of God.

In 1992, I had just given birth to our first child and found myself feeling completely overwhelmed. At 22 years old, I was a newly married woman, a recent college graduate, and unemployed. Kavin and I were struggling financially, and the weight of our situation was heavy. I knew I needed to find a job to help support our growing family, but I was filled with anxiety and self-doubt, unsure of my ability to balance everything. While I understood the importance of nurturing our baby, I also knew I needed to contribute financially to help provide for our family in this new chapter of our lives.

I can't say for certain that my husband and I had specific conversations about my postpartum experience, but I believe we had reached a deep level of understanding in our marriage that allowed him to sense when something was off with my emotional well-being. Without needing to ask, he began encouraging me, praying with me, and offering extra help around our small apartment. He was also just there to listen, offering his presence in the ways that mattered most.

I vividly remember one moment: after a long day of work, he came home with job postings he had found at the library. There were two counseling positions that matched my qualifications. I applied for both, and to my surprise, I received two offers. In the end, I chose the position with the best schedule, one that would allow me to care for our child while also spending more time with my husband.

I can't fully express the depth of my gratitude or the overwhelming sense of being loved and supported by my husband. In that moment, I realized how his role as my partner meant I was never alone in whatever journey I had to face. His support was the help I needed, and I felt the very presence of God working through him to lift me from a low place. A husband who truly loves his wife shows that love by investing in her growth and happiness, creating a space where she feels secure and valued. This kind of love goes beyond material provision, to include knowing her well enough to meet her needs in a holistic way and caring for her emotionally, spiritually, and mentally as well.

The Bible reminds us that marriage is a partnership of equals, built on a beautiful balance of mutual respect and shared purpose. In 1 Peter 3:7, husbands are instructed to "live with their wives in an understanding way, showing honor . . . since they are heirs with you of the grace of life." This verse underscores the fact that husbands and wives stand side by side, equally sharing in God's grace and purpose for their lives. Marriage is not a hierarchy, but a partnership where both partners are honored and valued as equals, working together to fulfill God's plan.

When a husband truly values his wife's journey, he doesn't view her goals or aspirations as secondary or lesser than his own. Instead, he becomes her biggest cheerleader, wholeheartedly supporting her whether she's pursuing a career, engaging in ministry, dedicating herself to creative work, or nurturing their children. He recognizes that her path is just as important as his, and he lifts her up with encouragement and respect.

Husbands are able to serve and support from this perspective because they've made the effort to dwell with their wives "according to knowledge," the idea that speaks to the importance of understanding their wives on a deep level. When a husband knows his wife, he becomes attuned to her temperaments, her emotional needs, her attitudes, and even her unspoken concerns. This knowledge allows him to offer love and support that is thoughtful, intentional, and genuinely helpful. It means he is not just reacting to surface-level issues but engaging with her heart and mind. By deeply understanding her, a husband can serve her in a way that strengthens both their individual journeys and their shared purpose as a couple.

Forgiveness, the Extension of Love

The Apostle Paul emphasizes the importance of forgiveness in Christian love. In Colossians 3:13, he writes, "Bear with each other and forgive one another if any of you has a grievance against someone. Forgive as the Lord forgave you." Paul's instruction is clear: the basis for our forgiveness of others is the forgiveness we have received from God. I am always baffled how we want forgiveness from the Lord, but we refuse to forgive others. In Ephesians 4:32, the Apostle Paul reinforces this again, "Be kind to one another, tenderhearted, forgiving one another, as God in Christ forgave you."

The Apostle Paul himself embodied this grace. In his earlier life, as Saul, he was responsible for persecuting the early church, but after his conversion, he experienced the grace of God firsthand. This grace not only transformed his life but also became a central message in his writings. Paul's journey from a persecutor to an Apostle shows how powerful forgiveness can be and serves as a reminder that we, too, are called to forgive and extend grace to others.

I am by no means suggesting that forgiveness is the easiest thing to do. While Scripture is clear about the need for forgiveness, it is also realistic about the difficulty of doing so. Human pride, pain, and the desire for revenge can make forgiveness seem impossible at times. Yet, it is precisely in those moments of struggle that God's grace becomes most evident. In my own struggle with forgiving those who had offended me, I would hear the Holy Spirit audibly asking, "Do you love me? (check). Are you professing to be a Christian witness? (check). Is the Bible your final authority?" (check). If all of this was so, why was I unwilling to forgive and release my offender?

I'm reminded of a passage of Scripture in Luke 17:4–5 that illustrates just how challenging forgiveness can be. Jesus tells His disciples, "Even if a person wrongs you seven times a day and each time turns again and asks forgiveness, you must forgive." The Apostles said to the Lord, "Show us how to increase our faith." This response from the Apostles was classic. It demonstrates that they understood that forgiveness, especially for repeated offenses, requires a level of faith beyond human strength. For them, the idea of continually pardoning every offense, regardless of the frequency, seemed daunting. Recognizing this, they didn't simply ask for more understanding of the offenders; they didn't even ask for more patience to cope with the offenses. Instead, they asked Jesus for greater faith, knowing that only through God's help could they meet such a high standard of grace.

Similarly, the Apostle Peter once asked Jesus how many times he should forgive a brother who sins against him. Jesus replied, not merely seven times, but "seventy times seven" (Matthew 18:22), emphasizing that forgiveness should have no limits. Peter's question led to one of Jesus' most impactful teachings, the parable of the Unforgiving Servant (Matthew 18:21–35). In this story, a servant who owes his master an enormous debt—so vast it's outside his ability to repay (NLT says millions of dollars)—is shown mercy and forgiven. However, this same servant turns around and refuses to forgive a fellow servant who owes him only a small amount in comparison (NLT says a few thousand dollars). Jesus' parable highlights the vast difference between God's boundless forgiveness and our often-limited willingness to forgive others.

The parable presents a striking irony. The servant with the smaller debt begged for mercy using the same plea that had saved the servant with the larger debt, yet it was all in vain, as the forgiven servant had him thrown into prison. This scene reveals the hypocrisy of asking God for forgiveness while refusing to extend it to others. For both spouses and believers, it's a reminder: we can't rightfully ask God for what we're unwilling to give ourselves. Jesus concludes the parable with a serious warning: those who withhold forgiveness from others will face judgment. The lesson is clear—Christians are called to forgive generously and without limits, just as God has graciously forgiven us.

Just imagine husbands and wives quickly overcoming misunderstandings and offenses as acts of love for one another and obedience to God. When we truly love, we do not keep count of the offenses by our spouses. Neither can we honestly say we forgive, yet there's tension between us.

I give God all praises and glory for His patience, mercy, and understanding toward me daily. Each day we all fall short whether through sins of commission or omission. Yet, God continues to extend love, protection, provision, and grace as if we have not overstepped or transgressed His law. His forgiveness toward us is our greatest example of what unconditional love looks like. Yes, God understands the difficulty of forgiveness, but He desires us to follow His example, which is why He provided the Holy Spirit to help us bear the fruit of love, grace, and forgiveness (Galatians 5:22–23).

If you really think about it, how can we not forgive and love, when our first experience with each of these was from God. 1 John 4:19 reminds us, "We love because he first loved us." Our ability to forgive flows from God's love for us. When we meditate on the enormity of God's grace, how much He has forgiven us, it becomes easier to extend that same grace to others, even when it feels difficult.

The story of Joseph is one of the most compelling examples of love, grace, and forgiveness in the Bible. As a young man, Joseph was betrayed by his own brothers, sold into slavery, and unjustly imprisoned. Yet, instead of allowing bitterness to define him, Joseph's faith in God remained strong. Years later, after he rises to a position of authority in Egypt, he finds himself in a position to either take revenge or extend grace when his brothers come to him seeking food during a famine. At that critical moment, Joseph responds not with vengeance, but with forgiveness. "You intended to harm me, but God intended it for good," he tells them, recognizing that God used his hardships to bring about a greater purpose (Genesis 50:20). Joseph's ability to forgive reveals not only his trust in God's sovereignty but also his understanding that mercy is a powerful force for restoration.

Joseph's story serves as a profound reminder of the transformative power of forgiveness within a relationship. In marriage, hurt and misunderstandings will arise. But just as Joseph forgave those closest to him, spouses can choose to extend grace instead of holding onto resentment. Joseph's choice to forgive healed deep familial wounds, restored broken relationships, and created an environment for love to flourish. Imagine the impact of applying this same grace within a marriage, choosing forgiveness over anger, understanding over judgment. Forgiveness in marriage doesn't just repair isolated conflicts—it builds a foundation of trust, emotional security, and unity. Joseph's story encourages couples to view their relationship in light of God's purposes, understanding that even challenges can serve to strengthen their bond when they're met with love, mercy, and forgiveness. In choosing grace, couples can experience deeper connection and healing, ultimately reflecting the kind of unconditional love God extends to us.

Yet still, the ultimate example of forgiveness and grace is demonstrated by Christ Himself during His crucifixion. Amidst the unimaginable pain and suffering on the cross, Jesus prayed for His executioners, saying, "Father, forgive them, for they know not what they do" (Luke 23:34). In this profound moment, Christ reveals a love that goes beyond human anger and bitterness. Even when faced with betrayal, violence, and injustice, He responds with compassion and extends grace to those who have wronged Him. This extraordinary act serves as a powerful example for believers: if Christ could forgive those who nailed Him to the cross, we too are called to forgive those who have wronged us in lesser ways. His example challenges us to rise above resentment and embrace a love that reflects His own—one that heals, restores, and transforms even the most painful relationships.

Forgiveness in a Christian marriage is a powerful reflection of Christ's love. When one spouse forgives the other for a hurtful word or a careless action, they extend the grace that not only heals but also strengthens the marital bond. This act of forgiveness embodies the unconditional love on which marriage vows are based, reminding both partners of their commitment to love beyond faults. Forgiveness creates a path for reconciliation, restoring trust and unity.

Without forgiveness, relationships remain tangled in frustration, resentment, and bitterness, clouding our vision and hardening our hearts. Trying to move forward without forgiving someone who has hurt you is nearly impossible; the hurt creates walls of defensiveness and distance. But forgiveness smooths over these rough places and clears away resentment, making space for restoration and genuine peace. In marriage, forgiveness is not just a one-time act but an ongoing choice essential to living out the genuine love that Christ calls us to demonstrate.

Just as Christ forgave us completely and without condition, we are called to forgive others. Through biblical examples like Jesus on the cross, Joseph's mercy toward his brothers, Paul's own transformed life, and the Apostle's clarification about forgiveness, we see how forgiveness is a powerful testimony of God's love.

The Husband's Protection

The biblical call for a husband to protect his wife is seen throughout Scripture, reflecting his roles as priest, prophet, and king within the home. This protective love is grounded in a Christ-like devotion that seeks his wife's well-being in all dimensions of life. As a priest, he is called to protect his wife and family in prayer, understanding that his role is to stand in the gap for her, interceding as Christ intercedes for the church. In Job 1:5, we see a glimpse of this priestly duty when Job offers sacrifices for his family, seeking God's favor and forgiveness on their behalf. In a similar way, a husband, acting as the priest of his household, regularly prays for his wife, covering her with God's grace and seeking His wisdom to guide their life together.

For years, my husband has been faithfully leading our marriage through daily prayer. We never leave the bed without first communing with God, offering up our hearts and petitions to Him as we start our day. While we both agree in prayer, my husband typically takes the lead, guiding us in our time of intercession. This routine is not just a practice but an act of service and protection, setting the tone for everything that follows. Prayer aligns our hearts and minds, reminding us that God is our ultimate source and foundation. Its power stands in its ability to shift any negative emotions or thoughts that might have lingered from the night before and to establish peace within our spirits.

This sacred time of prayer doesn't just prepare us for the day ahead, it also guards us against unseen spiritual battles. As we pray together, we are declaring God's dominion over every area of our lives, renouncing any negative or demonic attacks that may have come in through our dreams or thoughts. Through this daily intercession, we strengthen our spiritual unity, staying in harmony as we speak with one voice. By starting our day in prayer, we are able to maintain a sense of peace, clarity, and purpose, with our hearts firmly anchored in God's promises and our marriage continually fortified by His grace.

In the husband's role as priest, this means that he goes to God on behalf of his family. This priestly assignment places the spiritual tone of the home on the husband's shoulders. In 1 Peter 3:7, husbands are instructed to treat their wives with honor as co-heirs in the gift of life, so that their prayers may not be hindered. This verse highlights the gravity of a husband's role as a spiritual protector. His relationship with his wife is directly connected to his relationship with God, and how he treats her impacts his own prayer life. This encourages him to promote an atmosphere of respect, unity, and godliness that both honors his wife and strengthens their bond with God. As priest, he creates a sanctuary where both he and his wife can grow in faith, undistracted by discord or resentment.

When considering the role of the prophet, it is the prophet's responsibility to go to the people on behalf of God. Synonymously, the husband's responsibility includes speaking truth and encouragement into his wife's life. A biblical example of this is seen in Proverbs 31, where the virtuous woman's husband praises her at the city gates, publicly acknowledging her worth. This prophetic role involves affirming his wife's God-given identity and calling. It includes pronouncing a blessing upon her and giving her the counsel of God as needed. In Hebrews 3:13, believers are encouraged to "exhort one another daily" to prevent their hearts from hardening to sin. Likewise, a husband speaks encouragement to his wife, helping her see her value in Christ and her unique purpose. By recognizing her strengths and gifts, he helps guard her against self-doubt and discouragement, protecting her inner peace and sense of worth.

The prophetic role also means a husband must be attuned to God's voice, seeking guidance not only for himself but for his wife and family. In John 10:27, Jesus says, "My sheep hear my voice, and I know them, and they follow me." A husband listens to God's leading and shares it with humility and care, ensuring that his guidance aligns with God's will and not merely personal preference. Physical protection is the most basic form of security. However, spiritual protection will cover the family physically, financially, and emotionally. When husbands pray, they are seeking God's wisdom on life's decisions, thereby guarding their wives from instability or impulsive actions that may bring harm.

The role of the king brings the duty of stewardship and provision into a marriage. In Proverbs 27:23–27, men are reminded to know well the condition of their flocks, emphasizing diligence in managing their resources. For a husband, this translates into responsible leadership in financial and household matters. Rather than dominating, a God-fearing husband seeks to create a secure and well-provided environment where his wife feels protected and supported. This kingship mirrors the heart of Christ's kingdom—a servant leader whose priority is his family's well-being over his own comfort.

In this kingly role, a husband must also protect his home from external threats, whether they be financial hardships, emotional challenges, or influences that may disrupt family harmony. In Nehemiah 4:14, Nehemiah urges the people to "fight for your families, your sons and your daughters, your wives and your homes." Similarly, a husband stands as a protector, watching over his household and ensuring that nothing harmful disrupts their unity. As the king of his castle, a husband must protect his queen, his prince, and his princess from anything that threatens their security and well-being. He has to be vigilant and wise, discerning God's divine will for his home and taking steps to protect his wife from any negative influences.

Finally, a husband's role as protector includes accountability. In James 5:16, believers are encouraged to confess their sins to one another, highlighting the value of transparency. A husband who is not transparent and chooses to hide behind secrecy, whether it's locked phones, private calls, or fabricated business meetings, is not fit to lead his wife and family. In marriage, a husband must protect his relationship with God and his wife by living with integrity, guarding his marriage against deception and moral compromise. His commitment to accountability demonstrates deep respect for his wife, reassuring her that he values and honors their covenant with God and with one another.

Together, the roles of priest, prophet, and king encapsulate a husband's multifaceted duty to protect his wife in every way. By embracing these responsibilities, he embodies a Christ-centered love that serves, honors, and cherishes his wife, creating a marriage where she feels genuinely safe and deeply loved.

The Wife's Marital Role

The idea of a "biblical role" for a wife can sound a bit old-fashioned or even intimidating, but it's actually about something pretty timeless: building a strong, respectful, and loving partnership. At the heart of it is a mix of values like submission, respect, and partnership, but maybe not in the way we'd initially think.

In the Bible, submission isn't about being less than or giving up who you are. Instead, it's about trust and teamwork, choosing to support each other in a way that brings out the best in both partners. It's like learning to dance— sometimes you take the lead, and sometimes you let your partner guide, but the goal is always to move together in harmony.

Respect is another big part of this, and it goes both ways. Respect is about honoring each other's strengths, understanding each other's needs, and creating a space where both husband and wife feel valued. It's the glue that keeps things together, especially in tough times.

Finally, partnership is where it all comes together. Marriage is a shared journey, a space for growing together, and it's built on both partners giving their all to create a life they love. This chapter will dive into what these qualities look like in real life and why they still matter today. Let's take a look at how these principles can make marriage a place of joy, growth, and connection.

A Wife's Submission

"Wives submit yourselves unto your own husbands, as unto the Lord. For the husband is the head of the wife, even as Christ is the head of the church: and he is the savior of the body."

(Ephesians 5:22–23, KJV)

Submission, in a biblical and Christian context, refers to the act of yielding or placing oneself under the authority or leadership of another, often in a way that respects God's design for relationships. It involves humility, cooperation, and a willingness to honor the role and responsibilities of the other person by embracing a posture of respect and deference, all while trusting in God's sovereignty and guidance.

In marriage, submission is often understood as a wife's voluntary choice to support and respect her husband's leadership, as outlined in passages like Ephesians 5:22–24. However, biblical submission is not a state of inferiority or passivity. It's not blind obedience or a wife under the control of her husband. But submission is mutual respect, love, and partnership, where both spouses recognize and value each other's contributions. It's about creating a loving, collaborative environment where both partners work together for the benefit of the union and to fulfill God's purpose for their marriage and family.

Imagine for a moment that you're part of a team—maybe a sports team, a company, or a group working toward a shared mission. On any team, people have different roles, and it's essential that each person's role is respected for the team to function well. Some are leaders, responsible for making final calls, while others may take on supportive roles, ensuring the vision is realized smoothly. Just as in these team dynamics, family life operates best when each member's role is clear and respected.

When the Bible calls wives to "submit" to their husbands, it can sound challenging or even uncomfortable in our culture, where we often equate submission with inferiority. But in the original Greek, the word translated as "submit" was actually a term borrowed from the military. It described a structure that allowed soldiers to work together as a united force, each person knowing their place in relation to the others. In an army, rank isn't a measure of a person's intelligence, talents, or worth. A private may indeed be smarter, more skilled, or kinder than a general, but to serve effectively, he respects the authority of the general's role. In like manner, submission in marriage doesn't reflect a wife's value or abilities compared to her husband's; it speaks to the importance of honoring God's design for family order.

This design is also visible from a sports perspective. In this regard, imagine the marriage as a sports team with a captain. The captain's job is to lead and make quick calls when needed. However, the captain isn't superior as a person or more valuable than the other players. But in order for the team to score and be effective, the team has to work together and follow the direction of the captain. Similarly, in a family, God has assigned the husband as the "captain," not because he is inherently more deserving, but because this role brings order to family life. The wife, as a partner, supports and strengthens that leadership, bringing her own wisdom, gifts, and insights to the marriage. Children, in turn, look to both parents, respecting them as the leaders of the family.

The concept of marital submission cannot be emphasized enough, as someone must take a subordinate role. Think of submission in marriage like the dynamic between a superhero and their trusted wingman. In any great superhero story, the main hero, whether it's Batman, Wonder Woman, or Iron Man, relies on a strong, capable partner by their side. The wingman (or wing woman) isn't weaker, less skilled, or any less valuable—they bring essential strengths, insights, and back up to the mission. In a similar fashion, the wife is that capable wing woman who contributes to the betterment of a healthy and thriving marriage. As Paul reminds us in Galatians 3:28, men and women are equal in God's eyes. That equality doesn't change, even as each takes on different roles in the relationship. Being equal doesn't mean being exactly the same—it just means that both have an important part to play that's necessary for the success of the team.

A biblical understanding of a wife's submission in marriage involves a loving and voluntary response to her husband's leadership, reflecting a partnership grounded in mutual respect and commitment. Submission in this context is not about hierarchy or coercion but rather reflects a deep trust in God's design for the marital relationship. Submission is an expression of a wife's support and respect for her husband's role, acknowledging that her support strengthens and encourages him in his own calling to love and lead the family. This principle finds roots throughout the Bible, emphasizing that submission is both a spiritual posture and a practical expression of love and respect.

In Colossians 3:18, Paul writes, "Wives, submit yourselves to your husbands, as is fitting in the Lord." Here, submission is presented as an action that aligns with a life dedicated to honoring God. The phrase "as is fitting in the Lord" reminds us that submission is not passive compliance but rather an active, thoughtful decision to respect and honor one's husband out of reverence for God. Wives are called to uphold and support their husband's godly leadership while maintaining a spirit of humility and love. It's quite difficult for wives to declare their reverence for God while fighting their husband's godly leadership.

Likewise, in 1 Peter 3:1–2, wives are encouraged to be submissive to their husbands "so that, if any of them do not believe the word, they may be won over without words by the behavior of their wives, when they see the purity and reverence of your lives." Here, submission is shown to have the power to influence and inspire, even to lead their spouse to the Lord. Submission reflects a wife's commitment to living out her faith with integrity, showing love and respect even in challenging circumstances. For example, if a husband is unsaved or resistant to spiritual practices, a wife can demonstrate her devotion to God by serving her unbelieving husband through acts of kindness, patience, and respect. By prioritizing her relationship with Christ and modeling godly character, her actions may soften his heart and spark curiosity about her faith.

A wife's submission in marriage is modeled after the Church's submission to Christ, an image that captures a relationship rooted in love, trust, and dedication. Just as the Church follows Christ out of gratitude for His sacrificial love, a wife's submission is a loving response to her husband's care and godly leadership. This posture reflects partnership, flowing from a place of security and trust in both her husband's role and God's design for marriage. This kind of submission acknowledges the husband's responsibility to lead his family with wisdom, humility, and love, while also recognizing the wife's role as a supportive partner who strengthens and complements him.

In Proverbs 31, we see a wife who embodies this biblical concept. The Proverbs 31 woman is not passive or voiceless; but she is industrious, wise, and strong, managing her household with skill and foresight. She engages in business, evaluates fields for purchase, and contributes to the financial well-being of her family. Her role is multifaceted, blending her responsibilities as a wife, mother, and businesswoman in ways that honor God and her family. Her submission is not a restriction, but a means of empowerment as her husband validates her contributions that lend to the family's success.

Her contributions enhance her husband's leadership, and together they build a home that reflects God's grace and design. Proverbs 31:11 states, "The heart of her husband safely trusts her, and he will have no lack of gain," showing that her husband trusts and values her deeply. In fact, her submission brings honor to her husband and their household, as the team is empowered to rise to unimaginable heights as there is no competition and fighting amongst the team members.

In the early years of my marriage, submission was a concept I struggled to understand and embrace. I was just 19, full of my own ideas, and often self-centered in my thinking. When my husband and I disagreed, I questioned why he seemed to have the final say in decisions while my thoughts and perspectives appeared overlooked. This misunderstanding of submission caused tension in our relationship, leading to unnecessary conflict and turbulence during those formative years.

At the heart of my resistance was a lack of understanding about what submission truly means in a biblical sense. I saw it as a loss of agency rather than what it truly is, a partnership rooted in trust, respect, and love. I didn't realize that submission is not about one person controlling the other—it's about submitting under God's design for marriage, where both husband and wife work together for the good of their relationship and family.

When I began to learn the meaning and art of submission, things started to shift. The conflicts that once dominated our early years started to diminish. We were no longer adversaries but partners, united in purpose. Communication improved, and we started listening to each other with open hearts. Decisions became less contentious, and our home grew more peaceful. Financially, we noticed an increase in provision, as our alignment allowed us to manage our resources more wisely and collaboratively. With fewer arguments and greater harmony, we had more time and energy to enjoy each other's company. Our marriage became a source of joy and fun rather than frustration and strife.

Submission in marriage opened my eyes to the beauty of God's design. It taught me the value of humility and trust, not just in my husband but also in God's ability to lead us through him. It also created space for my husband to grow as a leader, encouraged by my support and respect. At the same time, it gave me room to thrive within my own God-given role, as my voice and contributions were valued and appreciated in the context of our partnership.

Ultimately, a wife's submission is a testament to her faith and trust in God's plan for her marriage. It involves a willingness to uphold and encourage her husband, even as she remains a vital and strong partner within the marriage. It is an active choice to cultivate peace, unity, and trust. Submission also sets a tone of humility and mutual dependence on God within the marriage, encouraging both spouses to seek God's guidance and serve each other selflessly.

Examples of Biblical Submission

The Bible provides many examples of wives who showed loving, voluntary submission while still expressing their own strength and wisdom in marriage. These examples reveal that submission can be both active and supportive, a partnership in which both spouses honor each other's roles. Here are a few powerful examples:

Sarah and Abraham

Sarah is a classic example of a wife who supported her husband's leadership while remaining strong in her own right. When God called Abraham to leave his homeland and follow Him to an unknown place, Sarah willingly joined him on this journey, trusting both Abraham's leadership and God's plan (Genesis 12:1–5). Despite the challenges they faced, Sarah's faith and support strengthened Abraham. She voiced her thoughts and concerns openly, like when she laughed in disbelief at the promise of a child in old age (Genesis 18:12), yet she ultimately stood by Abraham and played a vital role in the story of God's promise.

Esther and King Xerxes

Though Esther's story primarily centers on her courage in protecting her people, she provides an example of honoring her husband's position while still exercising her influence. When Esther learned of the plot to destroy the Jews, she did not confront King Xerxes aggressively but approached him with respect and wisdom, even fasting and praying before speaking to him (Esther 4:16). She demonstrated that submission doesn't mean staying silent; rather, it involves choosing wise and respectful approaches, which allowed her to protect her people and earn Xerxes' favor.

Priscilla and Aquila

In the New Testament, Priscilla and her husband, Aquila, worked together as a powerful team in ministry. Priscilla is often mentioned first, suggesting her active role in their work (Acts 18:18, 26; Romans 16:3–5). She supported

Aquila's ministry and taught alongside him, but her respect for his role is evident. Together, they taught Apollos more accurately about Jesus, showing that submission doesn't exclude a wife from contributing her gifts, insights, and wisdom to a shared purpose.

Mary, the Mother of Jesus, and Joseph

Mary displayed submission to God and supported Joseph's role as protector of their family. When an angel appeared to Joseph, warning him to flee to Egypt to protect Jesus, Mary followed Joseph's lead without hesitation (Matthew 2:13–14). Mary's submission was grounded in her own strong faith and trust in God, and she played an active part in raising and protecting Jesus. Mary's life shows us that submission is a willing, faithful response to God's plan, even when it means stepping into the unknown with her husband.

Each of these examples highlights that biblical submission involves a blend of support, strength, and trust, rather than passivity or blind obedience. These women displayed their own faith, courage, and wisdom, and their voluntary submission was an active expression of respect, grounded in partnership and love.

How Independent Women Embrace Biblical Submission in Marriage

For many strong, independent women, the idea of submitting to their husbands can feel like walking a tightrope, balancing their own identity, abilities, and voice with the biblical call to honor their husbands' role in the marriage. Submission may seem counterintuitive to the qualities that have shaped them, qualities like resilience, independence, and leadership. But what if submission, rather than diminishing these qualities, could actually magnify them within the context of a marriage built on love and mutual respect?

In my 36 years of marriage, submission has not always come easily. While I had no issue honoring my husband (or so I thought), the concepts of submission and obedience were much harder for me to grasp. I didn't realize that by struggling to submit to my husband's leadership, I was not fully honoring him. To me, it felt unnecessary to obey someone who, like me, was still learning and growing—we were both just kids. I vividly recall standing at the altar, repeating the vows. When the preacher said, "To love," I repeated, "To love." When he said, "To honor," I echoed, "To honor." But then came the word "obey." I felt a wave of resistance deep within me, a visceral response that this would be a challenge in our marriage. Looking back, it's clear that my mindset shaped my reality, as Proverbs 23:7 reminds us: "For as he thinketh in his heart, so is he."

In retrospect, I realize that learning submission was not a smooth or easy journey, it was shaped through seasons of frustration, resistance, and deep self-reflection. It took time, and even more than that, it took wrestling with my own pride, my own insecurities, and the assumptions I'd held for so long. Submission, to me, had always seemed like a synonym for weakness, a yielding that I couldn't reconcile with who I was. I had spent so much of my life building a strong sense of self, learning to stand my ground, and valuing independence. How could I let go of all that?

But life has a way of teaching us things we're not ready for, and often it teaches through opposition. There were moments in my marriage where the tension grew thick; arguments over decisions, silent battles over who would have the final say. I pushed against the idea of submission because I couldn't see how it would strengthen me or our relationship. All I saw was the potential for losing myself, for being overlooked, for becoming invisible. And I wasn't prepared for that.

Over time, though, the resistance wore me down, but not in a way that weakened me. It was like refining gold, burning away the dross of my fears and misunderstandings until all that was left was clarity. I came to realize that submission wasn't about giving up my voice or my strength. It wasn't about becoming less. But it was about choosing a new form of strength; the strength to trust, the strength to honor, the strength to let go of control. It was about recognizing that in giving my husband space to lead, I was affirming his role, and in that affirmation, I was truly honoring him which in turn deepened our relationship. We began to work together in ways I hadn't imagined possible.

Through the opposition, I came to see submission as a practice of humility, one that required as much courage as anything I'd ever done. It was a path toward greater intimacy, one where both of us could shine, neither diminished but both lifted by our willingness to embrace God's design for our marriage. I learned that submission isn't about losing; it's about creating a bond where we're stronger together than we could ever be alone. And that lesson, hard-won and shaped by struggle, is one I now carry with gratitude.

I believe there are many strong, independent, and well-meaning wives who can relate to my experience. Like me, you may need to reframe your understanding of submission in a biblical sense. This requires letting go of worldly ideologies that often hold us captive to societal narratives and expectations. These narratives emphasize independence, strength, self-agency, and equality, all of which have their place, but often stand in contrast to the biblical principle of submission.

Submission, as taught in Scripture, does not ask wives to lose their identities or diminish their value for the sake of the marriage. Instead, it invites them to embrace something far greater than individual pursuits and accomplishments—it calls for trust in God's design for the greater good. By yielding to God's design, wives create space for their husbands to step into their role as leaders, while their strengths and abilities remain a powerful and supportive force in their shared journey.

This type of submission is a deliberate and courageous choice, especially in a society that rarely celebrates it. It challenges the cultural emphasis on self-reliance and autonomy by advocating for interdependence and mutual respect.

Consider this scenario: Sarah, a confident, successful woman, feels a deep responsibility to support her family both emotionally and financially. She is accustomed to making decisions independently and is highly capable in her career and personal life. Submission, for her, might mean taking a step back not from her strengths, but from her habit of shouldering every burden alone. By involving her husband in decisions and entrusting certain responsibilities to him, she's creating a partnership where they both share the weight. This doesn't make her less effective or productive, but it makes her wiser, as she learns to lean on her husband's leadership without forfeiting her own voice.

I learned this firsthand when it came to decisions about our children's education. With my husband often away at work, I naturally took charge of academic matters: school meetings, assignments, and everything in between. Over time, it became second nature for me to make these decisions without involving him. However, I started to notice that my husband seemed to take a backseat in areas where I had assumed full control.

One day, I decided to shift my approach. I began asking for his input, inviting his perspective as their father. Slowly but surely, he started engaging more, attending school meetings, helping with homework, and even taking the kids to special events. His role as their dad became much more visible, and I noticed how our children began turning to him for guidance and support in ways they hadn't before.

This shift was a tremendous relief for me. I no longer carried the pressure of having to do and be everything for our children's academic success. At the same time, I witnessed my husband grow into a more present and active father. His involvement didn't diminish my role as their mother, it complemented it beautifully. By making space for my husband to step into his role as a leader, I created a balance that allowed both of us to thrive in our unique roles while working together as a team.

Ultimately, resourceful women understand that true submission is a purposeful choice rooted in wisdom and strength. It's an intentional act of supporting their husband's role and vision for the family, not because they lack capacity or ability, but because they value the unity that comes from working as a team. Such a woman seeks to build her husband up without diminishing her own identity. She leverages her gifts, talents, and strengths to complement and enhance her husband's leadership, rather than competing with him. By actively uplifting and encouraging him, she strengthens his ability to lead with confidence and purpose. Her deliberate support becomes a powerful force, transforming not only her husband but their relationship as a whole.

The Wife's Respect

The Biblical Foundation of Respect

Respect is a central tenet of biblical marriage. In Ephesians 5:33, Paul writes, *"However, let each one of you love his wife as himself, and let the wife see that she respects her husband."* This verse highlights the unique responsibilities within marriage: husbands are called to love sacrificially, mirroring Christ's love for the Church, while wives are called to respect their husbands in ways that honor their role and strengthen the marital bond. While love and respect are complementary, respect often takes a nuanced and practical form that deeply impacts the dynamics of a marriage.

At its core, respect is about recognizing and affirming the husband's God-given role. This perspective is rooted in biblical principles, which establish the husband as the head of the household (Ephesians 5:23, 1 Corinthians 11:3). In this role, he is tasked with leading, providing, and protecting his family. When a wife respects her husband, she acknowledges the spiritual authority and responsibility God has placed upon her husband, and she affirms his position and supports him in fulfilling his role.

Ephesians 5:23–24

23 For a husband is the head of his wife as Christ is the head of the church. He is the Savior of his body, the church.

24 As the church submits to Christ, so you wives should submit to your husbands in everything.

1 Corinthians 11:3

3 But there is one thing I want you to know: The head of every man is Christ, the head of woman is man, and the head of Christ is God.

Luke 22:27

27 Who is more important, the one who sits at the table or the one who serves? The one who sits at the table, of course. But not here! For I am among you as one who serves.

Matthew 20:26

26 But among you it will be different. Whoever wants to be a leader among you must be your servant.

The verses above highlight the headship of Jesus Christ over the Church, emphasizing His sacrificial love, as He gave His life for it. Christ's death was an act of selfless service, and though He is the head of the Church, His headship is defined by His role as the Servant Savior. This serves as a model for the husband's role in marriage. As the head, a husband's leadership is not rooted in power or authority, but in sacrificial service, much like Christ's example.

In Luke 22:27, Jesus teaches that the one who serves is greater than the one who is served. Similarly, Matthew 20:26 reveals that leadership in the Kingdom of God is defined by servanthood: "Whoever wants to be a leader must be a servant." Thus, the husband's role as the head of the wife is defined by leading through service (servant leadership).

As the leading servant in the marriage, the husband takes the initiative to make sacrifices for the well-being of the family. When difficult decisions arise, he leads by example, being the first to serve, even when it involves personal sacrifice or discomfort. His leadership is characterized by humility and a willingness to lay down his preferences or desires for the good of his wife and family.

When the husband and wife are at an impasse in their decision-making, the husband, as the head, must ultimately make the final decision. However, this decision is not made in isolation or in an authoritarian manner. It is made with consideration for his wife's perspective, and with the heart of a servant, recognizing that his leadership means shouldering the responsibility to ensure the decision is made and implemented effectively.

When wives recognize, understand, and honor their husbands' role as the head of the marriage, they are often willing to release their personal stance on various matters. There's no need to fight tooth and nail about every problem, as she is trusting and supporting her husband in the decisions that he believes God is leading him to make for the overall well-being of the family. This respect involves trusting him with the responsibility of decision-making, knowing that the Lord is guiding the husband just as He guides the wife. For example, if a husband feels led to make a major financial decision for the family's benefit, the wife demonstrates respect by sharing her thoughts with grace and then supporting his leadership, even if it challenges her comfort zone.

Acknowledging and valuing a husband's efforts and contributions is a demonstration of respect. It is a form of gratitude that recognizes the hard work, sacrifices, and leadership he brings to the relationship, both in practical and spiritual matters. This type of respect is not contingent upon perfection. No husband is without flaws, and recognizing this is key. However, respect is given not because of his perfection, but because of the husband's commitment to serve his family and the wife's commitment to honoring the role God has ordained for him as a husband.

When a wife respects her husband, she will applaud the tasks he accomplishes and the decisions he makes. But in a greater sense, she'll respect him because she values his heart, his intentions, and the weight of the responsibilities he carries. This respect means noticing his efforts—both big and small—and communicating appreciation for them. For example, when a husband works hard to provide for his family, a wife might express gratitude for the financial provision and for the sacrifices he makes to obtain it. When husbands take the initiative to guide the family in prayer or to make decisions about the family's future, wives should acknowledge these efforts to be respectful of their husbands.

Respect is also shown by valuing the husband's contributions to the household, whether they are material or emotional. In many marriages, the husband contributes in different ways: through physical labor, emotional support, financial provision, or spiritual leadership. A wife's recognition of these contributions, especially when they might go unappreciated or unnoticed, strengthens the bond between them. Sometimes when husbands serve consistently and effectively, their sacrifices can go unacknowledged as wives take their husbands' service for granted. If your husband maintains the orderliness of the home, he should be respected for his effort and contribution. If he takes time to nurture the children, don't chalk it up to "that's the least he can do," but simply respect the effort and applaud the contribution.

In practical terms, respect often manifests in how a wife communicates with her husband. Words have immense power in a marriage, and respectful communication involves speaking with kindness, encouragement, and affirmation. Proverbs 18:21 reminds us that "Death and life are in the power of the tongue," emphasizing that a wife's words can either tear down or build up her husband. Too many wives express their dissatisfaction in the marriage by nagging and complaining, thinking this will change the situation. But a wife who is a true helpmeet (not a "hurt-me") will respect her husband by choosing words that edify him and affirm his strengths even in small matters. Just acknowledging something as simple as washing the car or helping around the house can go a long way in showing respect and creating a positive family atmosphere.

Respectful communication also includes speaking the truth in love as encouraged in Ephesians 4:15. Maintaining a respectful tone and engaging in open and honest conversations without undermining or demeaning one's husband accords respect. Even if the wife disagrees, she frames her concerns in a way that shows she values his perspective and trusts his intentions. Wives, you cannot speak to your husbands like children and in a condescending tone and not think it's going to weaken his self-esteem. This conduct is a form of "tearing down" your husband with disrespect. Proverbs 31:26 describes the virtuous woman as one whose speech is marked by wisdom and kindness, illustrating that respect is often conveyed through thoughtful and intentional words.

Respectful communication also extends to public interaction. A wife should take extra care to avoid insulting her husband, speaking negatively about him, or making jokes at his expense in the presence of others. This is hurtful behavior and makes others view your husband in a negative light. When a wife belittles her husband publicly or privately, it says a lot about her as a woman and the choice she made in her husband as the leader of their home.

Instead, when she desires to respect her husband, she will speak highly of him, honoring his character and reinforcing their partnership. Even praising him publicly or expressing gratitude for his efforts shows that she values him not only in private but also in the eyes of others. Saying something like, *"I'm so proud of my husband for all he does for our family, it's a blessing to have a man like him,"* demonstrates admiration and respect in a way that lifts him up and affirms his role. This public affirmation strengthens trust and shows others a picture of God's design for a loving and respectful marriage.

Moreover, respect in marriage is reflected in how a wife prioritizes her husband's needs, particularly his sense of belonging and being desired by her. This aspect of respect touches on the emotional and psychological aspects that affirm his identity as a husband and partner. Respect in this context acknowledges his need to feel seen, appreciated, and cherished for who he is and the unique role he plays in the marriage.

Everyone has a need to feel a sense of belonging and husbands are no different. A husband needs to feel that he is an integral part of his family and marriage, not merely someone fulfilling obligations. Respect in this area means involving him in decisions, valuing his input, and cultivating a shared sense of purpose. For instance, asking for his opinion on major family plans or making room for his preferences when setting household routines shows that his presence and perspective matter. This kind of respect creates an environment where he feels secure and connected to his family, knowing that his role is appreciated and irreplaceable.

Two of the most impactful ways a husband feels deeply respected are through being desired by his wife and her willingness to initiate affection. These actions speak directly to a man's sense of worth, masculinity, and emotional security in the marriage. A husband needs to know that his wife sees him as attractive, both physically and emotionally, and that her love for him is not out of obligation but out of genuine passion and affection. Compliments about his appearance, such as, *"You look so handsome today,"* or playful expressions of admiration, like, *"I love the way your smile lights up a room,"* communicate that she is still captivated by him.

An extension of a wife's expression of desire for her husband is her willingness to initiate affection. It's one thing for wives to say they desire their husbands, but taking the lead in creating moments of intimacy speaks volumes about their commitment and passion. For many husbands, physical touch and intimacy are closely intertwined with their emotional connection to their wives. When a wife initiates closeness, whether through a warm embrace, holding his hand, sharing a passionate kiss, or inviting intimacy in the bedroom, it reassures her husband of her love, attraction, and desire for him.

Wives should approach this area with wisdom and intentionality. When physical intimacy and affection are neglected in a marriage, it can create emotional and physical vulnerabilities, potentially opening the door to temptation or a breakdown in the relationship. Prioritizing physical connection as an integral part of marriage helps guard against these pitfalls and reinforces the sacred union that both spouses share. This proactive effort is a tangible expression of respect, love, and care, protecting the marriage while nurturing the husband's emotional and physical needs.

Beyond physical affection, expressing emotional desire also strengthens a husband's sense of respect. This involves taking time to understand his thoughts, dreams, and feelings and showing deference for the things that are innately important to him. When a wife desires to connect emotionally with her husband, she'll take the time to learn what he thinks and how he thinks. Every man has a unique way of processing situations, making decisions, and interpreting the world around him. By actively listening and observing, a wife can align herself with her spouse's mental processes. Proverbs 20:5 states, "The purposes of a person's heart are deep waters, but one who has insight draws them out." A wife demonstrates love and emotional desire when she becomes that "insightful partner," drawing out her husband's thoughts with patience and care.

Other actions that display a wife's respect is showing enthusiasm in the couple's shared moments. Attending a sports game together, watching a television show he enjoys, or providing undivided attention in areas that concern his heart are examples of expressing enthusiasm for the husband's interest. Showing enthusiasm for the things that your husband enjoys communicates that the wife wants to see her husband happy, that she prioritizes his interests and enjoys his company. These actions also reflect that she values their physical bond as an essential part of their relationship and that she cherishes him not only for what he does, but she loves him for who he is.

The Transformative Power of Respect

Respect is not just a marital obligation; it is a gift that a wife gives to her husband, her family, and herself. It empowers a husband to be his best self, strengthens the marital bond, and reflects God's design for relationships. Respect is rooted in trust. A wife must trust God's plan for the marriage and trust her husband's leadership, even if there are areas where he may need to grow or improve.

Respect also means being patient and understanding when a husband is growing in his role as the spiritual leader. Not every man will feel confident or fully equipped for this responsibility, especially if spiritual leadership wasn't modeled for him while growing up. A respectful wife doesn't criticize or diminish his efforts but instead offers patience and encouragement.

When a wife respects her husband, she is giving him the space to develop into the man God has called him to be. This may involve extending grace in moments of weakness, encouraging him in areas where he is struggling, and believing in his potential as a leader. It also means standing by him in times of uncertainty, trusting that he is doing his best to lead according to God's will. Respect requires grace. Just as a husband is called to love his wife sacrificially, a wife is called to respect her husband, even when he falls short. While extending respect may sometimes feel challenging, its benefits far outweigh the difficulties.

When a wife consistently shows respect to her husband, it has the power to transform both the man and the marriage. Respect affirms a husband's role as the leader and protector of the family. Men are naturally wired to crave respect—it is their primary love language, even if unspoken. When a husband feels respected, he is empowered to rise to the occasion, leading with greater confidence, responsibility, and love.

Conversely, a lack of respect can break a man. Disrespect communicates that he is inadequate or unworthy, which can lead to feelings of failure, resentment, and withdrawal. Over time, this dynamic erodes the foundation of the marriage. A man who does not feel respected may struggle to love his wife well, creating a vicious cycle of unmet needs on both sides. Wives must commit to the decision of building their husbands through respectful actions which can transform even the most challenging unions.

A Wife's Partnership

A wife's partnership with her husband is a divinely ordained relationship of mutual support, respect, and unity, where she works alongside him to fulfill God's purpose for their marriage, family, and shared mission while honoring his God-given role as the head of the household and submitting to him as unto the Lord.

This marital partnership does not relegate the wife to an insignificant role where her contributions are overlooked and devalued. But this partnership is an amalgamation of both spouses' unique gifts, insights, and strengths that are utilized to create a sacred union even in challenging and turbulent times.

Partnership means standing together through life's challenges. A wife can display a supportive partnership by creating a safe space for her husband to share his concerns and struggles. Men often feel societal pressure to suppress emotions, but a wife who actively listens without judgment and encourages her husband to express vulnerability serves as a powerful marital ally.

Partnership requires flexibility, especially during transitions like a career change, a move, or parenting challenges. A wife who adjusts her role to meet the needs of a given season, whether by stepping into the workforce temporarily, shouldering more responsibilities at home, or encouraging her husband to take a sabbatical, embodies the spirit of collaboration that biblical marriage promotes.

Toward the end of 2007, I began experiencing a pressing desire to go back into the marketplace. Kav and I were low on our finances and needed additional streams of income. At that time, Kav was working in ministry full-time, and I was volunteering in ministry, in the throes of completing my doctorate degree, and working part-time in my clinical placement site to complete my practicum hours. My plate was full, and I didn't feel like I could entertain another responsibility. As the months continued, the urges to find a secular job were more pronounced.

I knew the Lord was dealing with me to support my family in financial ways that I knew Kav's schedule could not accommodate. After much prayer and consideration, Kav and I agreed that it was the right time for me to return to work to help ease our financial burdens. At the start of 2009, I reentered the workforce, and this decision proved to be an incredible blessing for me and our family's financial stability.

Returning to the marketplace was a tangible expression of true partnership in our marriage. There were things my family needed, and I had the ability to secure them. Balancing ministry, work, and school was no small feat, but I embraced the challenge for the sake of my family's well-being. I refused to let the enemy burden my husband with this responsibility, knowing that his primary focus was the ministry. For him to thrive and give his best, he needed to be fully present: spiritually, mentally, and physically. By stepping into this role, I was not only supporting my family but also empowering my husband to pursue his calling wholeheartedly.

Kav and I navigated this challenging season together for four years. My decision to come alongside my husband and partner with him in safeguarding our family's financial stability was a crucial factor in keeping us afloat during those trying times. Even years later, when I ultimately decided to resign from the position, the foundation of the partnership we had established bore lasting fruit. The retirement package I received as a result of that season significantly shifted our financial trajectory, underscoring how our shared commitment to partnership paved the way for enduring blessings.

Another vivid area of partnership in my marriage was in our parenting practices. As a young couple, we set the tone for our marriage and how we wanted our children to be raised. We wanted our children to be raised in a Christian environment that was warm, supportive, and filled with love, support, and joy. We soon learned that children could be manipulative, choosing to go to the parent who would allow their desires to be fulfilled. Kav and I had to make some changes to our parenting and stand as a united front in decisions that were made. If one parent did not approve of an activity, the other stood with them. This level of partnership did not allow our children to undermine our decisions. Our children witnessed our unity in the home, and it reinforced our Christian faith.

Another profound example of partnership in my marriage was reflected in our approach to parenting. As a young couple, Kav and I were intentional about setting the tone for our marriage and creating a clear vision for how we wanted to raise our children. We desired a Christian home environment that was warm, supportive, and filled with love, joy, and encouragement. However, we quickly discovered that children can be quite resourceful, and at times manipulative, seeking out the parent most likely to fulfill their wishes.

Recognizing this dynamic, Kav and I made intentional adjustments to our parenting style. We committed to standing as a united front in our decisions. If one of us did not approve of a particular activity or request, the other would support that stance. This partnership in parenting sent a clear message to our children that they could not undermine our authority or create division between us.

By maintaining unity in our decisions, we established boundaries and consistency within our home, and we also reinforced the principles of our Christian faith. Our children witnessed firsthand the strength of our partnership, which served as a living example of love, respect, and unity in marriage.

When children witness their parents working together in harmony to follow God's will, it reinforces their faith and demonstrates that the teachings of the Bible can be applied and lived out in everyday life. Partnering with my husband nurtured our family's spiritual foundation and allowed me to witness his growth as a father and the spiritual leader of our home. This growth didn't happen overnight—it was cultivated through prayer, encouragement, patience, and intentional collaboration.

Wives have the unique opportunity to be instruments in God's hands, creating an atmosphere where both spouses are empowered to flourish in their faith and fulfill their God-given roles. By supporting and standing alongside their husbands, wives contribute to a Christ-centered home that honors God and nurtures the spiritual health of the entire family. This partnership exemplifies God's design for marriage, where love, respect, and shared purpose build a strong foundation for spiritual growth and unity.

Chapter Reflections

Healthy, harmonious homes are created when both husband and wife commit to living out biblical principles in their marriage. This begins with the husband, who is called to be the spiritual leader of the home. He must model Christ-like love, humility, and faithfulness, loving his wife as Christ loved the church. Such love is sacrificial, prioritizing the wife's spiritual and emotional well-being.

A husband also honors God by protecting and providing for his family, ensuring their physical, emotional, and spiritual security. By being diligent in their work, maintaining integrity, and creating a safe and loving environment, husbands fulfill their God-given responsibilities. Like Adam, who was tasked with cultivating the garden of Eden, today's husbands are called to tend to their gardens by nurturing their wives, encouraging their growth and well-being. Above all, the husband must maintain accountability to God in all actions, seeking His guidance through prayer, worship, and obedience to His Word.

The wife, too, plays a vital role in making the marriage honorable before God. Scripture calls her to submit to her husband as to the Lord, not out of inferiority, but as a voluntary act of respect and support for her husband's God-given leadership. She is to be a suitable helper, complementing her husband's strengths and supporting him in their shared purpose. In simple terms, marriage is like a team, with the husband serving as the captain and the wife as his devoted co-captain. Together, they look to the Lord as their guide, trusting Him to direct their union in ways that bless their family and bring glory to His name. The wife supports her husband by lovingly standing beside him, trusting God to lead him, while also encouraging and holding him accountable to God's divine plan for their marriage.

Together, the husband and wife must pursue unity, leaving and cleaving as the Bible instructs. This involves prioritizing their relationship above all others, including family, friends, or careers. Unity is strengthened through mutual respect, shared goals, and open communication. They must also practice forgiveness, extending grace to one another and seeking reconciliation during conflicts, reflecting God's forgiveness.

At the core of their relationship is a shared commitment to Christ, which means praying together, worshiping together, and encouraging each other in their faith. Their love should reflect the selfless, unconditional love of Christ, embodying patience, kindness, and a willingness to put the other's needs above their own.

By fulfilling these unique roles and working together to seek God's will, couples create a marriage that not only thrives but also glorifies God. This kind of marriage becomes a living testament to His design for love and unity, serving as a powerful example of a sacred covenant that honors Him.

Prayer

Heavenly Father,

We come before You with grateful and humble hearts, thankful for the beautiful covenant of marriage You have designed. You created us uniquely and gave us roles that reflect Your divine love, wisdom, and purpose.

Lord, help my spouse and me to reflect Your glory in our marriage. Teach us to communicate with kindness, to forgive with open hearts, and to serve each other selflessly. Let us not be swayed by the world's standards but remain steadfast in the truth of Your design for marriage. Let us remember that our union is sacred and holy unto the Lord. Give us the strength to carry out our roles with understanding, deference, and patience.

Bind us together with a love that cannot be broken, and strengthen us to face challenges as one, always relying on You as our foundation and guide. Lead us to grow closer to each other as we grow closer to You, fulfilling the divine roles You have given us in love and unity. We declare that our marriage is healthy, our home is harmonious and we pray that you be pleased with our covenant.

In Jesus' name, we pray, Amen.

PART TWO

Building Blocks for a Strong Marriage

CHAPTER 4

Origins, Observations, and Outcomes:
The Work of Communication

According to the *Journal of Marriage and Family*, couples who engage in positive communication behaviors, such as expressing affection and appreciation, tend to report higher levels of marital satisfaction. Conversely, negative communication behaviors, like criticism and contempt, are associated with lower marital satisfaction levels.

Effective communication is the heartbeat of a thriving marriage, shaping the way couples connect, navigate challenges, and nurture intimacy. It is not merely about exchanging words—it is about conveying emotions, intentions, and desires in a way that promotes understanding and strengthens the bond between spouses. As couples learn healthy communication skills, they are able to express their needs, connect with one another, resolve conflicts, as well as build a partnership where both individuals feel seen, heard, and valued, contributing to overall marital satisfaction.

Couples who master effective communication prioritize creating a safe space where both individuals can express themselves fully and authentically. They listen not just to respond, but to understand. They create an environment where it is safe to be vulnerable, to share fears and dreams, and to tackle challenges without fear of judgment or dismissal.

Unfortunately, in today's fast-paced, technology-driven world, couples are less intentional and are often finding themselves communicating in ways that are shallow or rushed. Text messages, social media, and quick check-ins may replace deeper, face-to-face conversations and can make it harder for couples to connect on a deeper emotional level, leading to feelings of isolation, misunderstanding, or neglect. With the growing emphasis on concepts like emotional intelligence, digital mindfulness, love languages, and empathic attunement, couples are now inspired to develop their relational skills in deeper and more meaningful ways.

Emotional Intelligence

Emotional intelligence, for instance, plays a crucial role in helping couples navigate conversations with empathy, self-awareness, and intentionality. This involves recognizing and managing not just your own emotions but also understanding and validating your partner's feelings. Couples who intentionally practice emotional intelligence often find it easier to handle misunderstandings and maintain emotional closeness, even in the face of disagreements.

At its core, emotional intelligence begins with self-awareness—the ability to recognize and understand your own emotions as they arise. When couples develop this skill, they become better equipped to pause and reflect before reacting, reducing impulsive responses that can lead to conflict. This awareness allows each partner to articulate their feelings clearly and calmly, creating an environment where both can feel safe expressing themselves. For example, instead of snapping in frustration, a spouse might say, "I feel overwhelmed right now and need a moment to process," which opens the door for constructive dialogue.

Self-awareness in emotional intelligence is the ability to recognize your thoughts, emotions, and behaviors and understand how they influence your interactions. It involves being honest with yourself about your triggers, strengths, and weaknesses, and acknowledging how your emotional state can impact your relationship. In the context of marriage, self-awareness allows a spouse to identify when they are feeling overwhelmed, insecure, or defensive, enabling them to address these emotions constructively rather than projecting them onto their partner.

Developing self-awareness often requires reflection and intentionality. Tools like journaling, mindfulness practices, or even seeking feedback from your spouse can help identify patterns in your emotional responses. For instance, a partner might notice that they become short-tempered when they're tired or stressed from work. By recognizing this, they can communicate their needs more effectively, such as saying, "I've had a rough day and might need some quiet time before we talk." This proactive approach prevents misunderstandings and creates space for the spouse to decompress before engaging in communication.

Self-awareness also enhances accountability in marriage. It prompts individuals to take responsibility for their actions and reactions, avoiding the common pitfall of blaming their spouse for every conflict. When you're self-aware, you're more likely to pause, reflect, and ask yourself questions like, "Am I responding out of frustration or truly addressing the issue?" or "How might my tone or words come across to my partner?" This level of introspection leads to more thoughtful, respectful communication, and creates an atmosphere where growth and connection can flourish.

Equally important is empathy, the ability to step into your partner's shoes and truly understand their perspective. This goes beyond hearing their words—it's about actively listening, seeking to first understand versus being understood, observing nonverbal cues, and responding in a way that shows genuine care. Empathy helps couples move away from a "me vs. you" mindset to a "we" mindset, where the focus is on resolving issues together. If one partner expresses frustration about a challenging situation with a close friend, rather than dismissing their feelings or immediately offering solutions, the other might respond, "That sounds really upsetting. What can I do to support you in this?" Such responses not only validate emotions but also deepen emotional intimacy by demonstrating attentiveness and understanding.

Emotional intelligence also involves managing emotions effectively, particularly during disagreements. It's easy for couples to let heated emotions take control, leading to unproductive arguments. What starts off as a simple comment could escalate into a full-blown fight because one or both spouses are sensitive and not managing their emotions. However, those who cultivate emotional intelligence skills learn to regulate their feelings, using strategies like taking a break to cool off or rephrasing criticisms into constructive feedback. Additionally, emotionally intelligent couples recognize the impact of their words and tone, striving to communicate in ways that build up rather than tear down. This intentionality helps prevent misunderstandings from escalating and encourages a culture of respect and trust. By incorporating emotional intelligence, couples can create a solid foundation for communication that nurtures their relationship, even in the most challenging moments.

Digital Devices and Technology

Another modern focus is the impact of technology on marital communication. Digital devices, while convenient, can often act as barriers to meaningful connection. Technology's impact on marriage extends beyond mere distraction; it also shapes how couples perceive connection and availability. While digital devices allow instant communication, they can also create a false sense of closeness. Texting throughout the day or liking each other's posts on social media might seem like meaningful interaction, but these exchanges can sometimes replace deeper, face-to-face conversations. Over time, reliance on surface-level digital communication can erode emotional intimacy, as couples may feel they are connecting when, in reality, they are avoiding more profound discussions. Creating intentional, device-free moments allows couples to move beyond digital convenience and engage in the kind of meaningful dialogue that builds trust and understanding.

Another significant issue is the role of technology in fostering emotional distance when used as an escape. In the earlier years of our marriage, my husband and I would turn to our phones and tablets to avoid discussing challenging topics or to unwind after a stressful day. We were not mindful that these inanimate devices were creating greater emotional wedges between us. Using technology occasionally is normal, but habitual use can point to deeper communication problems. A partner who is always scrolling through social media during dinner might unintentionally convey that they're not interested or engaged, making the other person feel ignored or unimportant. Couples can counter this by setting boundaries around device usage like "tech-free zones" or "screen-free hours" during important conversations or quality time, signaling that their relationship takes precedence over digital distractions. Research shows that couples who consciously set aside distractions during conversations report greater satisfaction and intimacy.

Even the unassuming television has the same potential to create emotional distance in marriages. Television is a popular pastime in America, and it may seem like an enjoyable form of entertainment, but it can unintentionally create barriers in a marriage when watched excessively or without consideration for a shared connection. Have you ever watched a movie, or two or three with your spouse and no one says anything about the movie throughout the entire time? Watching TV can become a passive activity that limits meaningful interaction, especially if it replaces opportunities for conversation or quality time. Couples who routinely default to watching shows separately or zoning out in front of the screen may find themselves emotionally distant, as the time spent together lacks intentional engagement. Even when watching the same program, failing to interact or discuss what's being viewed can lead to a sense of isolation rather than bonding. Striking a balance by setting limits on TV time or choosing programs that both partners can enjoy together and discuss can turn a potential barrier into a shared experience.

Similarly, video games can also become a source of tension if one partner spends excessive time gaming while the other feels neglected. Gaming can be highly immersive, leading to hours of distraction that might pull attention away from a spouse or shared responsibilities. There's nothing worse than working and cleaning around the house while your partner has been kicking back for hours on a video game. This imbalance can create feelings of resentment or frustration, particularly if one partner feels left out or unimportant compared to the game. On the other hand, gaming doesn't have to be a barrier; it can become a bonding activity if both partners are interested or willing to play together. Open communication about the impact of gaming on the relationship, combined with boundaries to prioritize time as a couple, can help ensure that hobbies like gaming do not detract from the marital connection but instead enhance it.

On a more positive note, technology can also serve as a tool to strengthen marital communication when used intentionally. Apps designed for couples such as those focused on shared calendars, task management, or even relationship-building exercises, can help partners stay organized and connected. Video calls during travel or sending thoughtful messages can maintain closeness when physically apart. The key is striking a balance by leveraging technology to enhance connection without letting it replace or hinder the deeper, personal interactions that sustain a thriving marriage.

Love Languages

The concept of the Five Love Languages, introduced by Dr. Gary Chapman in his book *The 5 Love Languages: The Secret to Love That Lasts*, has transformed the way couples understand and express love. Chapman identified five distinct ways people give and receive love: Words of Affirmation, Acts of Service, Receiving Gifts, Quality Time, and Physical Touch. Each person has one or two primary love languages that resonate most deeply with them. Understanding these languages within a marriage allows couples to communicate love in ways that their spouse truly values, fostering deeper connection and intimacy.

Words of Affirmation involve expressing love through spoken or written encouragement, compliments, or appreciation. A spouse who thrives on this love language feels valued when their partner acknowledges their strengths, efforts, or appearance. Phrases like, "I appreciate how hard you work for our family" or "You look beautiful today" can make a significant impact. Conversely, critical or dismissive words can deeply wound someone who prioritizes this love language, highlighting the importance of positive and affirming communication.

Acts of Service focus on actions that demonstrate care and support. For spouses who identify with this love language, helping with daily tasks like cooking, cleaning, or running errands is seen as an expression of love. These acts show a willingness to share the load and ease the other's burdens, creating a sense of partnership and commitment. However, neglecting responsibilities or failing to follow through on promises can leave these individuals feeling unappreciated or unloved.

Receiving Gifts as a love language is not about materialism but rather the thought and effort behind the gesture. A well-chosen gift, no matter how small, represents love and thoughtfulness to someone who speaks this language. It could be as simple as bringing home their favorite snack or surprising them with a heartfelt token. Neglecting special occasions or failing to put thought into gifts can be particularly hurtful for individuals who value this form of love.

Quality Time emphasizes undivided attention and shared experiences. For individuals who connect through this love language, spending meaningful time together, free from distractions, is vital. This could include deep conversations, shared hobbies, or simply enjoying each other's company. Partners who fail to prioritize time together or allow distractions like phones or work to interfere can unintentionally create distance in the relationship.

Physical Touch encompasses expressions of love through touch, such as hugs, kisses, or holding hands. For those who value this language, physical closeness provides reassurance, comfort, and connection. A lack of touch or a cold physical demeanor can leave these individuals feeling isolated or unloved. In contrast, consistent and affectionate touch strengthens intimacy and emotional security.

By identifying and understanding each other's love languages, couples can enhance communication and build stronger relationships. When couples take the time to learn and "speak" each other's love languages, they create a marriage that is both resilient and deeply fulfilling. When building a marriage that honors God, it is necessary that we learn to speak the language of our spouse and not our own. Keep in mind that you are your spouse's help meet, and they are yours, so there's no need to be self-serving. So be careful when utilizing the love languages that you're not speaking the language you enjoy as opposed to speaking the language your spouse prefers. For example, if your spouse loves physical touch and you enjoy receiving gifts, don't think you're communicating your spouse's language by purchasing a gift (that's your love language) while withholding physical affection and intimacy (that's your spouse's love language). In order to meet your partner's unique needs, it will require intentional effort on your part.

Apology Languages

Much like love languages, apology languages, emphasize the unique ways people express and interpret heartfelt apologies. Understanding these languages can help repair relationships by ensuring that the person receiving the apology feels genuinely valued and heard. Each language speaks to a different emotional need and learning them can deepen trust and generate reconciliation in marriages, friendships, and family dynamics.

Imagine a couple, Rachel and David, who had an argument about financial decisions. Rachel is deeply hurt, not just by the argument but by David's initial dismissal of her feelings. David genuinely feels remorseful but notices that simply saying "I'm sorry" doesn't seem to resonate with Rachel. It's in this moment they discover the concept of apology languages, which teaches them how to navigate forgiveness effectively.

Expressing Regret focuses on acknowledging the emotional impact of one's actions and conveying sincere sorrow for causing hurt. This apology language is less about explaining or justifying behavior and more about empathizing with the feelings of the person who was wronged. It involves admitting the harm done and expressing genuine remorse in a way that validates the other person's emotions.

Accepting Responsibility is about fully owning one's actions or words without excuses, deflection, justification, or minimizing the harm caused. It requires a clear acknowledgment of wrongdoing and its impact on the other person, creating a foundation of trust and respect.

This apology language is vital because it communicates to the offended party, especially in a marriage, that their feelings are valid and that the wrong-doer is willing to be accountable for their part in the situation.

By admitting fault without deflecting, the apologizer demonstrates respect for the injured party's feelings and builds an atmosphere of mutual understanding. This process eliminates the defensive barriers that often arise in conflicts and paves the way for reconciliation.

When a husband accepts responsibility for a mistake, he affirms his wife's worth by acknowledging the weight of his actions and their effect on her. Similarly, when a wife accepts responsibility for her missteps, she reinforces her respect for her husband's feelings. In both cases, it's a tangible demonstration of love, humility, and commitment to working through challenges together. This not only repairs the immediate harm but strengthens the bond of trust and respect within the marriage.

Making Restitution is an action-oriented language that demonstrates a willingness to repair the harm done, showing that the apology is more than just words. This approach acknowledges that words alone are sometimes insufficient, and that true remorse involves taking meaningful steps to address the pain or damage caused by one's actions. For many people, restitution affirms the sincerity of the apology because it shows a willingness to invest effort and resources into restoring what was broken.

This language ensures that apologies are not hollow but are backed by meaningful change. It challenges the apologizer to ask, "How can I make things right?" and to follow through with intentionality. For example, if a husband has been inattentive due to overworking, making restitution could involve adjusting his schedule to spend more quality time with his wife, thereby addressing the root of the hurt and demonstrating a commitment to change.

Making restitution builds trust because it turns an apology into a bridge for healing. It shows that the offending party recognizes the value of the relationship and is willing to do whatever it takes to restore harmony and rebuild the connection.

Genuine Repentance is an apology language that emphasizes a heartfelt desire to change one's behavior and avoid repeating the actions that caused hurt. It's not just about expressing sorrow for what has been done, but about demonstrating a commitment to growth and transformation. This language is deeply meaningful because it provides assurance to the offended party that the apology is not empty talk, but it is a catalyst for lasting change in the relationship.

The goal of genuine repentance is personal transformation. It's about the person taking ownership of their actions and committing to a change of heart, mind, and behavior to ensure they don't repeat the mistake. It emphasizes the emotional and moral shift necessary for long-term healing.

Requesting Forgiveness is a direct, vulnerable action in which the person who has wronged someone asks for their forgiveness. It involves acknowledging the offense and actively seeking the other person's pardon, not only for the wrong but also for the emotional pain caused. It implies that the person is asking for restoration in the relationship and is open to reconciliation.

Empathic Attunement

Empathic attunement plays a pivotal role in fostering meaningful and effective communication in relationships. It refers to the ability to deeply connect with and understand another person's emotional state, responding in a way that validates their feelings and experiences. In a marriage or close partnership, empathic attunement allows couples to bridge emotional gaps and create a sense of safety and connection. By tuning in to their partner's emotions, whether expressed through words, tone, or nonverbal cues, spouses can respond with compassion and support, which strengthens the marital bond.

One of the key aspects of empathic attunement is active listening, which goes beyond merely hearing words. It requires fully engaging with the speaker, giving undivided attention, and seeking to understand not only what they are saying but also the emotions behind their words. If your spouse returned home expressing frustration about work, empathic attunement would involve recognizing their need for support rather than jumping to solutions. A simple response like, "That sounds really stressful. I'm here for you," would validate their feelings and open the door for a deeper connection.

Empathic attunement also helps partners navigate conflict more effectively. Instead of reacting defensively or dismissing their spouse's concerns, an attuned partner seeks to understand the underlying emotions driving the disagreement. I've worked with countless couples who come to therapy focused on a single issue, yet the real problem often lies beneath the surface. The arguments and tension they experience are typically symptoms of deeper, unresolved emotions or unmet needs. This realization led me to coin the phrase, "It's not about the cup," highlighting that what's in the cup isn't the issue at hand, but it's often something beneath the surface.

Empathic attunement allows couples to look beyond the immediate conflict, truly hear their partner's concerns, and acknowledge the deeper struggles driving their reactions. Instead of engaging in arguments, it encourages a response of empathy, patience, and care. By doing so, couples can address the heart of the matter and strengthen their emotional connection rather than fueling division. This approach creates mutual understanding and reduces the intensity of conflicts. To illustrate, if one partner is upset about a missed dinner date, an attuned response might be, "I see how disappointed you are. I didn't realize how much this meant to you, and I'm sorry." Such moments of emotional recognition and validation can de-escalate tension and rebuild trust.

In essence, empathic attunement transforms communication from transactional exchanges into relational moments of connection. It allows couples to feel seen, heard, and valued, making it a linchpin of emotional intimacy and healthy communication.

Communication Patterns from Families of Origin

Communication serves as the cornerstone of any marriage. It shapes the way couples interact, resolve conflicts, express affection, and build intimacy. The patterns of communication that individuals bring into their marriages often originate from their families of origin (the family one grew up in). The family of origin usually establishes the framework for how many individuals express feelings, handle conflicts, engage in dialogue, and develop emotional connections with their partners.

From the very beginning of life, children are like sponges, soaking up the behaviors, attitudes, and interactions they witness within their home environment. This process of observing, absorbing, and eventually replicating what they see forms the foundation of how they will communicate and relate to others throughout their lives. These early experiences are more than just fleeting moments—they serve as a critical training ground for emotional intelligence, conflict resolution, and communication skills that extend into adulthood.

Children begin their education in communication by observing those closest to them, typically their parents or caregivers. Every interaction, whether it's a casual conversation, a disagreement, or a moment of affection, teaches them something about how relationships function. For example, a child who observes parents calmly discussing their feelings learns that open communication is safe and productive. Conversely, a child who witnesses yelling, avoidance, or unresolved tension may come to associate conflict with fear, discomfort, or instability.

This observational learning extends beyond verbal exchanges. Nonverbal cues like tone of voice, facial expressions, and body language are just as impactful. A loving touch during a disagreement can teach reconciliation, while an angry glare can instill fear or defensiveness. Over time, these observations shape the child's internal understanding of how relationships should operate.

The behaviors children observe aren't just seen, they are internalized and will usually be the outcome of their own communication style. A child who grows up in an environment where emotions are acknowledged and validated learns that feelings are acceptable and manageable. On the other hand, a child in a dismissive or emotionally unavailable home may internalize the belief that emotions are to be hidden or ignored. Over time, these absorbed behaviors become the default responses that children carry into their own relationships.

As children grow, they begin to replicate the communication styles they've absorbed, first with peers and later in adult relationships. These replications are often unconscious, reflecting the deeply ingrained patterns established during childhood. The replication stage becomes especially significant in marriage. Spouses often discover that their communication styles, shaped by their family of origin, may either complement or clash with each other. For example, one partner may expect open dialogue during disagreements, while the other prefers silence, leading to frustration unless both recognize the influence of their upbringing.

The communication patterns absorbed in childhood are like seeds planted in fertile soil. With time, they grow into habits that influence how individuals approach every relationship, from friendships to professional interactions to marriage. By understanding and addressing these early influences, individuals can break free from unhealthy cycles, cultivate stronger connections, and build relationships that reflect grace, empathy, and mutual respect.

Breaking Negative Communication Patterns

For those who grew up in challenging communication environments, it is important to recognize these patterns and actively work to change them. Breaking poor communication patterns in marriage is an intentional process that requires humility, self-awareness, and a commitment to change. This may require therapy, self-reflection, and intentional practice to adopt healthier communication behaviors.

While every relationship is unique, the journey toward better communication often begins with an honest assessment of what is not working. Couples must confront their communication habits, understand their origins, and decide to replace them with healthier alternatives. This transformation is not instant but unfolds gradually as trust is rebuilt and new patterns take root.

Below are some suggestions that can assist couples in breaking free from toxic communication styles.

Imagine a couple, Sarah and James, who have struggled with constant misunderstandings and arguments. Sarah often shuts down when she feels overwhelmed, while James becomes defensive and quick to anger. Both love each other deeply but recognize that their communication habits are driving a wedge between them. They decide to take steps toward change, beginning with self-reflection.

- **Recognize and Acknowledge the Problem**

  You must first recognize you have a problem with communication because you cannot conquer what you're unwilling to confront. One of the greatest challenges in rendering therapy is trying to counsel an individual who does not think they have a problem.

  In our scenario here, Sarah and James realize that their communication issues didn't develop overnight. James traces his defensiveness to a childhood where he often felt criticized, leading him to react with anger to protect himself. Sarah, on the other hand, grew up in a family where emotions were rarely discussed, so she learned to suppress her feelings rather than face conflict. By acknowledging these patterns, they start to see how their family of origin shaped their responses in adulthood.

  This recognition is crucial because it shifts the focus from blaming each other to understanding the deeper roots of their struggles. Instead of seeing each other as adversaries, they begin to view their communication issues as a shared challenge they must overcome together.

- **Commit to Change**

  Once you acknowledge the challenges you are having in your communication, commit to making the necessary efforts to experience change. Agree to establish ground rules for conversations, such as avoiding blame, using respectful language, and taking breaks if emotions run too high. These boundaries create a safe space for dialogue, reducing the likelihood of escalating conflicts.

  Decide to seek guidance, recognizing that you may need outside help to break long-standing patterns. Attend a marriage workshop at your church or in your community and begin meeting with a counselor who specializes in relationship communication. These resources can provide couples with tools to navigate their challenges and reinforce their commitment to change.

- **Practice New Skills**

  Whatever skills you are learning to cultivate healthy communication patterns should be utilized at this stage. Just because you are learning a new skill does not mean that old patterns will not emerge.

  For example: James comes home late from work without letting Sarah know, and she feels hurt and unimportant. In the past, Sarah would have withdrawn, and James would have dismissed her feelings as overreacting. This time, however, they approach the situation differently.

  Sarah begins by calmly expressing how she feels. "When you didn't call to let me know you'd be late, I felt like I wasn't a priority," she says, using "I" statements to take ownership of her emotions. James listens without interrupting, resisting the urge to defend himself. Instead, he acknowledges her feelings: "I can see why you'd feel that way, and I'm sorry for not communicating better."

This small interaction marks a turning point for them. By practicing empathy and avoiding their usual defensive or withdrawn behaviors, they create space for understanding and reconciliation.

- **Rebuild Trust**

  As you begin to practice healthier communication, you'll notice a shift in your relationship. Misunderstandings no longer spiral into major arguments, and you'll feel more connected and supported. However, you must also understand that breaking poor communication patterns isn't just about learning new skills—it's about rebuilding trust.

  Trust grows as you consistently show up for each other, even in small ways. If you're accustomed to shutting down and withdrawing when you're angry, make the effort to move past your feelings and do the needful by voicing your needs instead of shutting down. If you're normally defensive, try responding with kindness. Stop expecting different outcomes when you're still committed to the same behaviors. You must do something different, to get something different. Over time, these changes reinforce your commitment to each other, proving that you both are willing to invest in the relationship.

- **Create a New Standard for Your Family**

  As your communication improves, you'll notice the impact it has on your family. If children are present, they'll witness your respectful dialogue, learning how to express their emotions and handle disagreements constructively. What you received from your family of origin does not mean it has to be what your children receive from their family of origin.

  By breaking poor communication habits, you can transform your marriage from a source of frustration to a place of growth and connection. While the journey is not always easy, the rewards are profound, leading to a stronger marriage that honors God, blesses the couple, and inspires others.

Benefits of Healthy Communication in Marriage

- **Enhances Marital Satisfaction**

  Effective communication is vital for a successful marriage. Positive communication promotes emotional intimacy, strengthens bonds, and facilitates conflict resolution. Conversely, poor communication can lead to misunderstandings, emotional disconnection, and ultimately, marital dissatisfaction.

  Research consistently shows that couples who communicate well report higher levels of satisfaction in their relationships.

- **Builds Emotional Intimacy**

  Open and honest communication allows spouses to share their thoughts, feelings, and dreams, which promotes a deep emotional connection. Feeling understood and valued creates a sense of safety and closeness that enhances intimacy.

  However, if sexual challenges are present in the marriage, healthy communication is a must. Sexual issues not openly discussed, lead to misunderstandings and resentment, making it even harder for couples to address the issue together. Over time, the reduction in physical intimacy can weaken emotional closeness, leaving both partners feeling isolated and disconnected.

- **Resolves Conflicts Effectively**

  Every marriage faces challenges. Healthy communication helps couples address disagreements constructively rather than letting them escalate. By focusing on understanding and resolution instead of blame, couples can navigate challenges without damaging the relationship.

- **Enhances Trust and Transparency**

  When partners communicate openly, they build trust by showing that they are honest and transparent with each other. This mutual trust forms the foundation for a strong and lasting marriage.

- **Promotes Teamwork and Cooperation**

  Good communication encourages spouses to work together as a team. They can better align their goals, share responsibilities, and make joint decisions, ensuring that both feel supported and included.

- **Reduces Stress and Misunderstandings**

  Clear communication minimizes confusion and assumptions, which can lead to unnecessary stress. Discussing issues openly prevents minor misunderstandings from growing into larger problems.

- **Encourages Individual Growth**

  Healthy communication allows both partners to express their needs, aspirations, and boundaries. This mutual support helps each person grow individually while maintaining a strong partnership.

- **Creates a Positive Atmosphere**

  When couples communicate respectfully and lovingly, it sets a tone of kindness and understanding in the relationship. This positive dynamic makes the home environment more peaceful and enjoyable.

- **Improves Problem-Solving Skills**

  Regularly discussing and addressing issues together builds stronger problem-solving abilities. Couples who communicate well are better equipped to tackle life's challenges as a united front.

- **Supports Physical and Mental Health**

  Healthy communication reduces tension and emotional distress, which can benefit both physical and mental health. A supportive marriage often correlates with lower stress levels and a greater sense of well-being.

- **Models Positive Behavior for Children**

When couples practice healthy communication, they set a powerful example for their children, teaching them how to express themselves respectfully and resolve conflicts constructively.

Children raised in homes with healthy communication are more likely to develop strong emotional intelligence and relationship skills. In contrast, children from families with poor communication may struggle with expressing feelings and resolving conflicts later in life.

Chapter Reflections

The way we communicate as adults often stems from the lessons and patterns we learned in childhood. From an early age, individuals observe and absorb how their families express emotions, resolve conflicts, and engage in everyday conversations. These early experiences serve as the foundation upon which adult communication is built. Whether through direct observation or personal interaction, children learn how to approach difficult conversations, how to express their needs, and how to manage disagreements. For example, if a child grows up in an environment where their feelings are ignored or invalidated, they may struggle as adults to express themselves openly in relationships, or they may avoid confrontation altogether. Conversely, if a child experiences open, honest, and respectful dialogue, they may be more likely to cultivate these healthy communication habits in their adult life.

Recognizing that these communication habits are deeply rooted in early life experiences is an essential step toward improving relationship dynamics. By becoming aware of the communication patterns learned in childhood, individuals can identify the ways they may unintentionally repeat unhealthy behaviors.

Improving communication in marriage isn't just about resolving conflicts more effectively—it's about creating a culture of emotional safety, empathy, and connection. When couples understand the role early communication experiences play in their adult relationships, they can make intentional efforts to improve the way they speak and listen to each other. This might involve learning to express feelings without criticism, addressing conflicts with respect and understanding, or simply being present and attentive during everyday conversations. Over time, this conscious effort leads to stronger emotional connections, a more resilient partnership, and a deeper sense of mutual respect.

Prayer

Heavenly Father,

We come before You as two individuals united in marriage, seeking Your guidance and strength to communicate better with one another. Lord, You designed marriage as a sacred partnership, and we know that effective communication is essential to building a strong and loving relationship. We ask for Your wisdom to help us speak to each other with kindness, patience, and understanding.

Father, help us to listen with open hearts and minds, not just to respond, but to truly hear the thoughts, feelings, and needs of our spouse. Teach us to be slow to anger, quick to listen, and slow to speak. When we are frustrated or misunderstood, give us the grace to communicate in a way that brings peace and resolution, not division.

Above all, we ask that You continue to strengthen our marriage as we seek to honor You in every aspect of our relationship. May our communication reflect Your love, truth, and humility. Teach us to build a strong foundation of trust and intimacy through honest, open dialogue, and may we always seek to glorify You in the way we speak to and about each other.

In Jesus' name, we pray, Amen.

"Conflict doesn't ruin marriages; it's how we handle conflict that determines our success."

Dr. John Gottman

CHAPTER 5

Empathy, Encouragement, and Effective Exchange:
Conflict Resolution

Conflict is a state of disagreement, opposition, or struggle between two or more parties arising from differences in values, beliefs, needs, goals, or perceptions. It can manifest in various forms, ranging from internal conflict within an individual to interpersonal, organizational, or societal conflicts.

At its core, conflict occurs when the desires, expectations, or interests of one party clash with those of another, creating tension or discomfort. While often perceived negatively, conflict is a natural part of human interaction and can be constructive or destructive depending on how it is managed.

The Nature of Conflict in Marriage

Marriage is described in Genesis 2:24 as the joining of two lives into "one flesh," symbolizing the profound unity of husband and wife. However, this unity does not mean the loss of individuality. When spouses enter a covenant with one another, they each bring their unique identity, shaped by their past experiences, personal dreams, emotional wounds, and expectations for the future. While these differences enrich the marital bond, they also lay the groundwork for inevitable conflict.

Conflict in marriage is not a sign of failure or incompatibility. Things will go wrong, and you will not always agree or get it right, but it doesn't mean the marriage is a mistake. When conflict arises, it is a natural outcome of two distinct individuals navigating life together and each spouse bringing their unique perspectives to the relationship. For many, these differences in personality, upbringing, communication styles, and emotional needs will lead to misunderstandings and disagreements. However, it's essential to recognize that conflict is not inherently destructive, but the key lies in how these conflicts are approached and resolved.

The mind plays a central role in how we perceive and resolve conflict, particularly within marriage, where every disagreement becomes a crossroads. How we perceive, interpret, and respond to tension often determines whether we emerge stronger as a couple or more fractured. Understanding the mind's influence can transform not only how we approach conflict but also the outcomes it produces.

First, consider how the mind shapes perception and interpretation. Every experience in life is filtered through our thoughts. Past hurts, assumptions, and biases all converge to form the lens through which we view our spouse. Have you ever found yourself assuming the worst in a disagreement, convinced that your partner's actions were intentionally hurtful? There have been times I have accused my husband of ignoring my requests or neglecting opportunities to assist me in a task. His response has been, "If you think I am intentionally doing these things to hurt or overlook you, then you don't know me." Over time, I have come to recognize that these thoughts and beliefs that I was projecting onto Kavin were not the result of his intent. Instead, they originated from my own mind's tendency to fill in gaps with assumptions (e.g., believing he was ignoring me) and fears (e.g., that he was neglecting me). By understanding how my mind's narratives were distorting reality, I've been able to approach disagreements with greater clarity and compassion.

Perhaps in your own marriage, your partner forgot your anniversary and it felt like proof of neglect when, in reality, it was an honest oversight. You might think that forgetting the date of your anniversary equates to neglect, but that doesn't necessarily mean your spouse processes the situation the same way.

Our perceptions, shaped by the mind's internal narratives, can distort reality and create unnecessary strife.

The mind also governs emotional regulation, which is critical during conflict. When tempers flare and words are exchanged, it is the mind that decides whether we fuel the fire or extinguish it. A defensive mindset or one overwhelmed by frustration can spiral even minor disagreements into full-blown arguments. This is what some call "emotional hijacking."

Emotional hijacking occurs when strong emotions, such as anger or fear, override the mind's ability to think rationally. In these moments, we often say or do things that escalate the conflict rather than resolve it. During an emotional hijack, the part of the brain that processes emotions takes over the part that manages logical thinking and decision-making. This can cause a person to jump to conclusions, burst out in anger, shut down, or any other extreme emotional reactions (e.g., shaking, racing heart, increased blood pressure, fast breathing, etc.).

Another role of the mind in conflict is its attachment to beliefs and expectations. Every person enters marriage with a set of assumptions about what marriage should look like and how their spouse should behave. Sometimes, these beliefs are unrealistic, rooted in cultural narratives or personal fantasies. For example, believing that your spouse should instinctively know your needs without you ever expressing them is a common but flawed expectation. We've all had those moments where we expect our spouse to know how we feel about a situation, to know how we think about an issue, to know how to respond to a problem without being informed. While such expectations may seem natural to you, they are often unrealistic and can lead to unnecessary frustration. When these expectations go unmet, conflict frequently arises, not because of what actually happened, but because of what we believed should have happened.

The Wisdom of Ephesians 4:26–27 (NIV)

Conflict in relationships, especially within marriage, is inevitable. Two people coming together, each with unique backgrounds, personalities, values, and expectations, will naturally encounter disagreements. In fact, the Bible does not warn against conflict itself, but rather guides us in how to handle it.

In Ephesians 4:26–27, the Apostle Paul advises, "In your anger do not sin: Do not let the sun go down while you are still angry, and do not give the devil a foothold." The scriptural implications are that you will become angry at one time or another. However, if your anger isn't processed appropriately, you'll carry it into another day. This verse is a profound reminder of the potential dangers of unresolved conflict.

Today, the importance of addressing conflict is more critical than ever. Divorce rates remain high, and many couples cite unresolved conflict, communication breakdown, and accumulated bitterness as significant factors. For the home, the family, and society as a whole, learning to handle conflict in a healthy, biblical manner has powerful implications. We live in a fast-paced, stress-filled world where instant gratification is common, but nurturing patience and empathy is not. As a result, many couples feel overwhelmed and unprepared to handle marital conflict.

Ephesians 4:26–27 (NIV)

26 "In your anger do not sin": Do not let the sun go down while you are still angry,

27 And do not give the devil a foothold.

Apostle Paul's words offer a three-fold approach to handling conflict:

- Do not sin in anger.
- Resolve issues quickly.
- Guard against the devil's influence.

Do Not Sin in Anger

The command "In your anger do not sin" (Ephesians 4:26) speaks to the fact that anger itself is not inherently sinful. It is a natural and legitimate human emotion—one that can arise in response to injustice, hurt, or frustration. God, who created us in His image, made us capable of experiencing a wide range of emotions, including anger. Even Jesus Himself displayed anger at times, most notably in the episode where He drove the money changers out of the temple (John 2:13–17). This act of righteous anger was motivated by a deep sense of justice and reverence for God's house, and it was in no way sinful.

However, the Bible is clear that it is not the anger itself that is sinful, but rather what we do with that anger. The danger lies in how we allow our anger to shape our actions, words, and attitudes. When anger is not managed properly, it can easily lead to sin. James 1:19–20 declares the following:

> 19 "Understand this, my dear brothers and sisters! Let every person be quick to listen, slow to speak, slow to anger.
>
> 20 For human anger does not accomplish God's righteousness."

Uncontrolled anger can lead to outbursts of wrath, bitterness, harsh words, and even a desire for vengeance; behaviors that can harm others and break relationships.

In a similar way, anger can be compared to fire. Fire, in its proper context, can be a source of warmth, light, and purification. It can refine and purify metals, provide comfort and warmth, and illuminate the darkness. Anger, too, when channeled properly, can motivate us to take righteous actions, speak up for those who are oppressed, and work for justice. It can be a powerful force for good when it prompts us to address wrongs and seek restoration.

On the other hand, unchecked fire can be destructive, consuming everything in its path, leaving devastation behind. Similarly, when anger is not controlled, it can cause great harm. It can lead to hurtful words spoken in the heat of the moment, deepening wounds rather than healing them. It can create division, stirring up strife, bitterness, and even hatred. Relationships can be torn apart when anger is not tempered with love, patience, and self-control.

God calls us to a higher standard. He doesn't want us to suppress our anger or pretend it doesn't exist, but He does call us to be mindful of how we handle it. Rather than letting anger control us, we are called to control our anger. This means taking a step back before reacting, reflecting on our emotions, and considering the impact our words and actions will have. It means choosing forgiveness over revenge, reconciliation over division, and understanding over judgment.

Resolve issues quickly

The instruction "Do not let the sun go down while you are still angry" (Ephesians 4:26) carries profound wisdom for maintaining healthy relationships, especially within marriage. At its core, this verse identifies the importance of addressing conflict promptly, rather than allowing anger to fester overnight. When anger is not addressed, it can give way to resentment, bitterness, and miscommunication, of which each can erode trust and intimacy between partners.

The longer a conflict is left unresolved, the more room it has to distort perceptions, cloud judgment, and create emotional distance. In marriage, where emotional bonds run deep, unresolved anger can be particularly destructive. When couples choose to let anger go unaddressed, it creates space for negative emotions to grow, often in ways that are disproportionate to the original issue. For example, one partner feels that their thoughts and feelings aren't being listened to during conversations, but they don't voice it directly. Over time, the unaddressed frustration builds up. The partner may start withdrawing during discussions or becoming increasingly defensive when speaking. What began as a minor irritation of feeling unheard becomes a significant issue that undermines emotional intimacy, leading to feelings of neglect and emotional disconnection.

Unresolved conflict leads to resentment, as one or both partners feel unheard, disrespected, or undervalued. This resentment, if left unchecked, can eventually lead to greater misunderstandings and a breakdown of communication. It's easy for small irritations or disagreements to become much larger issues when they aren't confronted and worked through. Another example of this can be when one partner makes a large purchase without consulting the other, causing tension, but it isn't addressed directly. As more unspoken financial decisions are made, the partner who feels left out becomes more upset. What started as a small irritation grows into distrust over financial decisions. Eventually, this can lead to arguments about money, with one partner feeling that their opinions don't matter, and the other feeling criticized for their choices. The disagreement now involves deeper issues of control, trust, and respect.

By committing to resolve conflicts before the end of the day, couples demonstrate a shared responsibility for maintaining the health of their relationship. This commitment is not simply about "fixing" every issue immediately but about showing care for one another and prioritizing the relationship over personal pride or stubbornness. It is a decision to face discomfort together, to engage in difficult conversations with the goal of understanding and reconciliation. In doing so, couples affirm that their connection to each other is more important than the temporary satisfaction that might come from being "right" or winning an argument.

I'm not suggesting that every conflict can or should be resolved in a single night. Some issues are complex and may require time, reflection, and thoughtful discussion. The goal is not to force an immediate resolution, but to take the first steps toward healing. Acknowledging the conflict, expressing one's feelings, and committing to continue working toward resolution are crucial elements of this process. It means agreeing to not let anger harden into something more damaging by the end of the day, and instead choosing to stay engaged and open to working through the issue together.

This practice requires humility and vulnerability from both partners. Humility because each person must be willing to admit their own faults and shortcomings in the conflict and be open to the possibility that they may have contributed to the situation in ways they hadn't considered. Vulnerability because it calls for emotional honesty, both in expressing anger and in sharing the deeper feelings that often lie beneath it, such as hurt, fear, or disappointment. For many couples, this is one of the most difficult aspects of conflict resolution, as it requires them to let down their guard and allow themselves to be emotionally transparent with one another.

By addressing conflicts early, couples also create a pattern of behavior that builds trust. It shows that they are committed not just to the relationship in the abstract, but to the ongoing work of maintaining that relationship. This is especially important in a marriage, where long-term commitment is often tested by inevitable disagreements. The decision to address issues promptly reinforces the understanding that the relationship is a shared responsibility and that both partners are equally invested in its success. It is an ongoing practice of reconciliation, choosing to forgive, to listen, to empathize, and to prioritize peace.

Importantly, this principle helps foster a mindset of unity rather than division. In a marriage, when couples work together to resolve conflict, they communicate that they are not adversaries but partners, and that their commitment to each other is stronger than any temporary emotional response. This mindset transforms the way couples approach conflict, shifting from a "me vs. you" mentality to a "we vs. the problem" approach. In this way, even disagreements can become opportunities for growth and deeper connection.

Guard against the devil's influence

Finally, Paul's warning, "Do not give the devil a foothold," speaks to the spiritual repercussions of unresolved conflict. Bitterness, grudges, and resentment create fertile soil for negative influences. The devil seeks to divide, weaken,

SACRED UNIONS IN TURBULENT TIMES

and ultimately destroy what God has joined together. When couples allow bitterness to take root, they open the door to division and estrangement.

The warning of not giving the devil a foothold (Ephesians 4:27) is a call to protect the sacredness of marriage by vigilantly rooting out the seeds of resentment. Paul's warning carries significant spiritual weight, especially when applied to the context of marriage. The concept of a "foothold" in this passage refers to an opportunity or a space where the enemy can gain influence and access. In the context of unresolved conflict within a marriage, this foothold often comes in the form of bitterness, grudges, and resentment. These negative emotions, if left unresolved, are spiritual vulnerabilities that the devil can exploit to create division and harm within the marriage.

When couples fail to address conflict in a healthy way, they may unknowingly open the door to spiritual attack. The Bible teaches that our hearts and minds are battlegrounds in the spiritual realm. Ephesians 6:12 states, "For we are not fighting against flesh-and-blood enemies, but against evil rulers and authorities of the unseen world, against might powers in this dark world, and against evil spirits in the heavenly places." The enemy is looking for any and every opportunity to destroy what God has blessed. The devil's ultimate goal is not merely to create disagreement or tension between spouses, but to tear apart the sacred covenant that exists between them. In marriage, the enemy seeks to divide, weaken, and destroy, knowing that a unified couple is a powerful force for God's Kingdom.

A word of caution: when bitterness, resentment, grudges, and the likes, manifest themselves in your relationship, recognize them as warning signs of danger. The devil thrives in environments where the works of the flesh are in operation, using these negative emotions as tools to sow division and discord. When such feelings are allowed to take root, they become fertile ground for the enemy's influence.

The longer resentment remains unaddressed, the more it festers, growing and spreading like a toxin. What might start as a minor hurt or misunderstanding can quickly spiral into deep-seated anger, a desire for revenge, or emotional withdrawal. Hebrews 12:15 warns that bitterness can "defile and corrupt many." This means its impact is not limited to the individuals involved but it can spill over into the relationship, damaging trust, intimacy, and mutual respect. The enemy delights in this kind of discord, for he knows that the longer conflict and disunity persist, the weaker the marriage becomes in resisting his attacks.

The Impact of Conflict in the Family

The way a couple handles conflict directly affects the entire family. Children, in particular, observe and internalize these dynamics, shaping their own approach to conflict resolution. When parents handle disagreements with respect, empathy, and forgiveness, they model healthy conflict resolution, preparing their children to build healthy relationships in their own lives. Conversely, when children witness unresolved anger, harsh words, or silent resentment, they may come to view conflict as something destructive or frightening, potentially carrying these unhealthy patterns into their own relationships.

Moreover, the health of a marriage influences the spiritual atmosphere of the home. A home filled with unresolved conflict and bitterness creates an environment of anxiety and insecurity, where family members may feel constantly on edge. Children in such an environment may internalize the conflict in various ways. Some may act out, become anxious and others may even blame themselves for the discord they sense. Even spouses themselves can become emotionally exhausted, as the unresolved tension chips away at their mental well-being and erodes their ability to connect with one another and their children.

In contrast, in a home where conflicts are handled with grace, patience, and love, an entirely different atmosphere is developed—one of peace, safety, and spiritual growth. When spouses prioritize healthy communication, quick forgiveness, and reconciliation, they model these virtues for their children and create a sense of stability. Family members feel secure knowing that while disagreements may arise, they will be addressed constructively and without lasting harm to relationships.

Practical Steps for Healthy Conflict Resolution

1. **Address Conflict Early:** Instead of letting disagreements fester, couples should make a conscious effort to discuss issues before they escalate. This may mean taking time to listen, reflect, and communicate with patience and humility.

2. **Choose Forgiveness:** Perhaps the most profound role of the mind in conflict lies in its ability to choose forgiveness and renewal. Forgiveness is not just a feeling but a choice. Couples must decide to forgive one another, even when it's difficult, and not allow unresolved issues to cloud their view of each other.

   Many conflicts persist not because of the original disagreement but because the mind clings to grievances. Resentment, replayed over and over in our thoughts, strengthens its hold, making reconciliation feel impossible.

   Yet forgiveness begins in the mind, often long before it is felt in the heart. It is a deliberate choice to release the offense and refuse to let it define the relationship. Philippians 4:8 offers guidance for this renewal: "Whatever is true, whatever is noble, whatever is right, whatever is pure, whatever is lovely, think about such things."

   By focusing the mind on what is good and honorable in our spouse, we can shift away from conflict's negativity and toward reconciliation.

3. **Seek Reconciliation, Not Victory:** The aim of conflict resolution in marriage should not be to "win" the argument, but to restore harmony and understanding. Both partners should focus on finding common ground and ensuring that the relationship is strengthened rather than strained.

4. **Pray Together:** Praying together during or after a conflict can be a powerful way to invite God's presence into the relationship. It not only reminds couples of God's power to heal and restore but also invites unity by aligning them with a shared purpose. Prayer softens hearts, helping couples to see their spouse through God's eyes.

Prayer is a necessary weapon in spiritual warfare. Couples should make a habit of praying together, seeking God's help in overcoming division, and asking for His strength in forgiving one another.

5. **Guard the Heart:** Resolving conflict in marriage begins with the heart, as Proverbs 4:23 wisely counsels: "Above all else, guard your heart, for everything you do flows from it." This verse highlights the profound connection between the condition of the heart and the words, actions, and decisions that follow. In the context of conflict, guarding the heart means being intentional about what we allow to take root within us, whether it's bitterness, pride, or resentment, and choosing instead to cultivate love, grace, and kindness.

When a couple faces conflict, the heart becomes a battleground. Hurt feelings, misunderstandings, and unmet expectations can tempt individuals to hold onto bitterness or nurture a desire for retaliation. Left unattended, these emotions can harden the heart, making reconciliation difficult. Bitterness, like a weed, grows rapidly and can choke out the love and compassion necessary for healthy communication. Proverbs reminds us that the heart is the source of all our actions; if the heart becomes tainted, it will inevitably influence our behavior and the way we approach conflict.

Guarding the heart requires vigilance, especially in the heat of disagreement. It involves recognizing and rejecting the lies that often accompany conflict—lies like "They don't care about me" or "They'll never change." These thoughts, though subtle, can poison the heart, turning a simple misunderstanding into a deep-seated grievance. Instead, couples must choose to fill their hearts with truths rooted in God's Word: that love is patient, kind, and not easily angered (1 Corinthians 13:4–7), and that forgiveness is not optional but essential (Colossians 3:13).

6. **Practice Active Listening:** In moments of conflict, listening is often overshadowed by the urge to speak, defend, or justify. Active listening, truly hearing what one's partner is saying, requires patience and humility. It involves pausing, focusing on the other person's words, and resisting the urge to interrupt. Proverbs 18:13 reminds us, "To answer before listening, that is folly and shame." When couples listen without judgment, they show respect and demonstrate that they value each other's feelings.

7. **Communicate with Kindness and Respect:** Ephesians 4:15 advises believers to "speak the truth in love." This principle is invaluable in marriage. While honesty is crucial, it must be tempered with compassion. Avoiding accusatory language, focusing on "I feel" rather than "You always" or "You never," helps to create an atmosphere where each partner feels safe to express themselves.

8. **Seek Understanding, Not Victory:** Many people enter conflict with the subconscious goal of proving themselves "right." But in marriage, winning an argument at the expense of one's partner is a hollow victory.

   Couples must shift from seeing each other as adversaries to viewing themselves as teammates. When both spouses seek to understand the other's perspective, they build a foundation of empathy, even if they cannot fully agree on a specific issue.

Chapter Reflections

Conflict is an inevitable part of life, especially in close relationships like marriage. Far from being a defect, conflict reflects the individuality of each partner and the natural differences in perspectives, experiences, and desires. When viewed through this lens, conflict becomes less about opposition and more about opportunity, a chance to better understand and grow together.

The nature of conflict often stems from unmet needs, unspoken expectations, or emotional wounds. While disagreements can feel disruptive, they also hold the potential to reveal deeper truths about our own hearts and those of our partners. By approaching conflict with humility and a desire to learn, couples can navigate disagreements in ways that strengthen their bond rather than weaken it.

Ephesians 4:26–27 offers timeless wisdom for managing conflict. "Be angry, and do not sin; do not let the sun go down on your anger and give no opportunity to the devil." This passage highlights three key principles: anger itself is not sinful, but it must be handled in a way that honors God; unresolved anger can fester into bitterness, so addressing issues quickly is vital; and harboring anger or unresolved conflict can open the door to destructive influences that harm the relationship.

To avoid sinning in anger, couples must practice self-control and intentionality. While anger is a natural emotion, how it is expressed determines whether it brings healing or harm. Allowing anger to simmer or erupt without reflection often leads to words and actions that deepen wounds. Instead, Scripture encourages a balanced approach: acknowledge the emotion, but respond with grace and wisdom.

Resolving issues quickly is another essential component of healthy conflict management. Delaying resolution allows misunderstandings to grow and emotions to harden, making reconciliation more difficult. By addressing issues promptly, couples demonstrate a commitment to unity and a willingness to confront challenges head-on, strengthening the foundation of trust.

Guarding against the devil's influence means being vigilant about the ways unresolved conflict can harm a marriage. Bitterness, resentment, and division are not just emotional consequences—they are spiritual vulnerabilities that can destroy intimacy and trust. A heart focused on reconciliation and forgiveness is one that resists these destructive forces.

Practical steps for healthy conflict resolution include clear communication, active listening, and prioritizing unity over personal victory. Couples should seek to understand each other's perspectives, express their own needs without blame, and work together to find solutions that honor both individuals. Prayer, humility, and a commitment to God's truth provide the foundation for navigating conflict in a way that reflects love and respect.

In summary, conflict, when approached with wisdom and intentionality, can transform relationships. By following biblical principles, addressing issues swiftly, and resisting divisive influences, couples can turn disagreements into opportunities for deeper connection and spiritual growth. Marriage is not the absence of conflict but the pursuit of unity through it.

Prayer

Heavenly Father,

We come before You today as a couple, seeking Your guidance and wisdom in casting out conflict and division in our marriage. We acknowledge that in our human nature, we can sometimes let emotions get the best of us, and misunderstandings can arise. But we trust in Your Word, which teaches us to be slow to anger, quick to listen, and always ready to forgive.

We ask for the strength to resolve conflicts in a way that strengthens our bond rather than tearing us apart. Guide us in finding solutions that are in alignment with Your will for our lives and marriage. May we honor You through our actions, reflecting Your grace and mercy in every situation.

In Jesus' name, we pray, Amen.

CHAPTER 6

Tenderness, Trust, and Togetherness:
Connection and Intimacy

Intimacy and connection are at the heart of a God-honoring marriage, serving as the foundation for a deep, enduring bond between spouses. This chapter delves into the significance of cultivating both emotional and sexual intimacy, emphasizing that true connection goes beyond the physical aspect to encompass a profound understanding and sharing of each other's innermost thoughts, feelings, and dreams.

Scripture offers guidance for couples creating this connection, with passages like Ecclesiastes 4:9–12 illustrating the strength and support that come from a close partnership: "Two are better than one, because they have a good return for their labor: If either of them falls down, one can help the other up. But pity on anyone who falls and has no one to help them up. Also, if two lie down together, they will keep warm. But how can one keep warm alone?" This passage highlights the practical and emotional benefits of intimacy in marriage.

Building intimacy requires effort and intentionality. It involves regular, open communication, shared experiences, and the cultivation of trust and vulnerability. Couples are encouraged to spend quality time together, engage in meaningful conversations, and actively listen to each other. Additionally, prayer and spiritual connection play a crucial role in deepening the marital bond, aligning the couple's hearts and purposes with God's will.

Cultivating Emotional Intimacy
Vignette

Mary sat by the window in her cozy study, gazing at the garden where the last bit of sunlight lit up the roses. Sitting there quietly, she began contemplating on the deeper emotional intimacy that had been quietly woven into her relationship with Matthew over the years. It was during these moments of reflection that she realized how her understanding of sex had evolved beyond the physical act to something much richer: it had become an integral expression of their emotional connection.

For Mary, emotional intimacy with Matthew had always been a quiet, ongoing journey. It wasn't just about passionate nights or fleeting moments of closeness, it was the consistent nurturing of their bond, the small gestures of kindness, and the shared vulnerability that made their marriage something sacred. As she thought about the intimate moments shared between them, she saw how each time they came together—whether it was through conversation, a shared laugh, or physical closeness—it was a reaffirmation of their connection. They weren't simply connecting in the physical sense; they were strengthening the invisible thread that tied them emotionally.

She thought about the power of shared vulnerability, how it had transformed their relationship. There were times when they had opened their hearts to each other in ways they hadn't before expressing fears, unmet needs, and unspoken hurts. In those moments, sex was no longer just about pleasure—it became a profound expression of trust and mutual care. They were not just "making love," they were making space for each other's souls to merge, creating emotional intimacy that went far beyond the physical.

Mary understood now that emotional intimacy was the soil in which their physical intimacy could truly flourish. The trust they had built through years of conversations, the kindness they had shown during difficult times, and the grace they extended to one another formed the foundation of their sexual connection. Without that emotional safety, she realized, physical intimacy would have felt hollow. It was the deeper connection of the heart that made their lovemaking truly powerful, making them "one flesh" in both body and spirit.

The reflection on their journey together deepened Mary's appreciation for what they had. She recognized that emotional intimacy was not something that happened by accident, it was something they worked at, intentionally nurturing each other through love, forgiveness, and grace. She thought back to their early years, when their passion felt effortless, and how now, in the midst of life's challenges, their intimacy was still present but required more intentional effort to maintain. But that effort was exactly what made their connection even more meaningful.

Mary realized that just as physical intimacy requires care and attention, so does emotional intimacy. It wasn't enough to have love on a surface level—they had to dig deeper, allowing themselves to be vulnerable and open with each other about their fears, desires, and needs. Only then could they experience the full depth of connection that God intended for marriage. This was why sex was so significant—it wasn't merely a physical act, but an intimate reflection of the trust and love they shared on every other level.

As Mary thought about all of this, she felt a sense of peace wash over her. She knew that their journey toward deeper intimacy, both emotional and physical, was far from over, and yet she felt confident in their ability to navigate it together. They had the foundation of trust, vulnerability, and shared love to build upon.

Sex, in her mind, was just one of the many ways they communicated their love for each other. It was a beautiful act of surrender, an exchange that reinforced the unity they had cultivated over the years. And just as emotional intimacy had required effort and intentionality, so too would their sexual intimacy continue to evolve as they grew together in their marriage. Each new phase of their journey would offer new opportunities to deepen their bond and express their love in fresh and powerful ways.

As she prepared for bed, Mary smiled, realizing that their sexual intimacy was far more than just an act, it was a deep, powerful reflection of their connection, vulnerability, and love for one another. And that, she thought, was the beauty of it: the sacred, ongoing journey of becoming one in body, soul, and spirit.

Emotional intimacy is the foundation upon which all other aspects of a relationship are built. It involves deep trust, vulnerability, and connection on a soulish level. In a marriage, emotional intimacy begins with shared experiences, both joyful and challenging, and it grows over time as both partners invest in each other's hearts. It's the safety to express one's fears, desires, and dreams, and the comfort of knowing that your spouse will listen with empathy and understanding.

True emotional intimacy requires constant nurturing. It's showing up for each other in the daily challenges that create moments of closeness and unity. Emotional intimacy includes the quiet conversations, the shared burdens, and the small acts of kindness that knit the hearts together in oneness and love. When couples actively seek to understand each other's emotional needs and communicate openly, they create a space where love can thrive and deepen.

When the emotional foundation is strong, sexual intimacy becomes a powerful vehicle for expressing love, affection, and commitment.

Cultivating Sexual Intimacy

Sexual intimacy is not an isolated act; it is a reflection of how emotionally connected a couple feels. I encourage couples to start making emotional, mental, and spiritual connections early in the morning that often leads to physical connection at night. When spouses invest in emotional closeness, they create an atmosphere of trust and vulnerability that naturally leads to deeper physical connections.

Each morning, my husband and I start our day together in prayer. Before stepping out of our bedroom, we take time to pray for protection and guidance. We ask God to bind any unseen spiritual attacks that may have occurred during the night or that the enemy may attempt to bring into our day. We pray for safety in our travels, protection over our children, blessings over our ministry, and care for our loved ones and those in need.

We also pray specifically against confusion, division, or any tactics the enemy might use to drive a wedge between us, whether through family, friends, finances, or other challenges. In doing this, we are actively "commanding our day" in alignment with Job 22:28, "You will also decree a thing, and it will be established for you; and light will shine on your ways." By starting each day in the spirit, we set the tone for unity, clarity, and God's protection over every aspect of our lives.

I encourage you to invite God into every part of your marriage, including its sexual intimacy. Welcoming His presence brings a sacred dimension to this area, aligning it with His purpose for your relationship. When you pray together as a couple, you open your hearts to divine guidance, which can help you navigate personal and relational struggles.

Praying together also strengthens your spiritual bond, creating vulnerability and trust. This deeper connection reduces barriers like fear, insecurity, and emotional distance, which lends to a safe and loving environment where both spouses feel valued and desired. A spouse who feels spiritually supported and emotionally nurtured is naturally more open to physical expressions of love.

Sexual intimacy begins long before you enter the bedroom. A partner who has been spiritually neglected or emotionally dismissed during the day may find it difficult to give themselves fully at night. By intentionally cultivating connection through prayer, affection, and understanding throughout the day, you create the foundation for a more meaningful and satisfying physical relationship.

In addition to emotional and spiritual intimacy, acts of affection also contribute to creating a solid foundation for cultivating sexual intimacy. Acts of affection such as hugs, kisses, gentle touches, texting loving messages, phone calls, spending lunch time together, leaving notes, etc. throughout the day create a sense of closeness that naturally leads to greater sexual connection.

These nonsexual behaviors foster warmth and build a bridge to sexual desire. When affection is constant, sex becomes constant. Lovemaking becomes a continuation of the loving connection rather than a separate, pressured act.

Husbands and wives, it is your responsibility to make time for your marriage and one another. Life's busyness often causes couples to neglect physical and sexual intimacy, so it's necessary to make time for physical connection. When there are work, home commitments, coupled with children, ministry obligations, and possibly school and extracurricular activities, something will be overlooked—and all too often, it's the marriage. Scheduling time for connection ensures that sex remains a priority. As couples prioritize their times of intimacy, they become keener to distraction and are more inclined to set healthy boundaries that have the potential to encroach upon your quality time.

At the very least, couples need to communicate their unique desires and personal preferences for healthy, sexual intimacy. Honest conversations about likes and dislikes, or what feels meaningful in the sexual relationship promote connection and anticipation. When spouses feel free to discuss their fantasies, timing, and even their challenges within the relationship, it increases the couple's level of comfort, making their sexual encounters more enjoyable and fulfilling.

A strong and fulfilling marriage requires both husband and wife to feel understood and valued. This begins with being attentive and responsive to each other's needs and preferences. If your spouse has expressed discomfort or dislike for certain behaviors, touches, or approaches, it's crucial to respect their boundaries and adjust accordingly.

Marriage is a covenant of mutual service, where each partner prioritizes the needs of the other. As Paul writes in Ephesians 5:21, "Submit to one another out of reverence for Christ." This means setting aside selfish desires and focusing on how to love and serve your spouse effectively. When both partners adopt this mindset, their needs are met naturally through mutual care and selflessness. Replacing selfishness with a desire to serve transforms the relationship. Trust, intimacy, and deeper connection are developed, creating a marriage where both partners thrive.

Sexual Disorders That May Affect Sexual Intimacy

Sexual disorders involve significant challenges with desire, arousal, orgasm, pain, and overall sexual functioning. These difficulties can affect not only physical intimacy but also emotional connection and marital satisfaction. However, it is important to remember that, as couples of faith, sex is a divine gift designed to deepen the bond between husband and wife. Approaching these challenges with patience, grace, and a shared commitment to work through them together can transform difficulties into opportunities for growth and intimacy, strengthening your marriage in the process.

Below are listed various sexual disorders that offer potential solutions to remedy the ailment. Although each disorder offers psychological, behavioral, and medical solutions, should any of these issues arise, you should first employ prayer for healing, patience, wisdom, and guidance as you navigate any challenge together. A focus on biblical principles of love, grace, and partnership (e.g., Ephesians 4:2) can build unity during the healing process.

The DSM-5 (Diagnostic Statistical Manual) categorizes sexual disorders into four main categories: 1) Sexual Desire/Interest Disorders 2) Arousal Disorders 3) Orgasmic Disorders 4) Pain Disorders.

Specific Sexual Disorders for Men

1. **DESIRE DISORDERS**

Male Hypoactive Sexual Desire Disorder (HSDD):

A persistent or recurrent deficiency (or absence) of sexual thoughts, fantasies, and desire for sexual activity, causing clinically significant distress and lasting for at least six months (with consideration for age and cultural context).

Potential Effects on Marriage:

The effects of this disorder are decreased intimacy making one's spouse feel alienated particularly if sex is highly prioritized in the marriage. It can also cause frustration, sadness, feelings of loss, and overall stress when the desire for physical and sexual connection for the wife is unmet by her husband. Another effect is the potential for misunderstandings about a lack of affection or attraction. When there's no intercourse in the marriage, spouses begin to wonder about their level of desirability and attractiveness to their partner.

Potential Solutions:

- **Psychological**: Address stress, anxiety, and any relationship conflict through counseling.

- **Behavioral**: Sensate Focus Exercises (Masters & Johnson) should be considered to gradually increase the intimacy in the marriage. Sensate Focus Exercises are used to improve intimacy and communication between partners around sex and sexual performance anxiety. It uses physical touch (non-erogenous and erogenous zones) to help build trust and intimacy within the relationship as each spouse learns about their own sensations as well as their partners. During these exercises, there's no expectation or pressure to become aroused, making it ideal for this sexual disorder.

- **Medical**:

  o **Hormonal Treatments** (e.g., Testosterone Replacement Therapy—TRT). TRT increases testosterone levels, which can help with sexual desire and erectile dysfunction.

    ▪ Gels—Testosterone can be administered through the skin by Gels (e.g., AndroGel, Testim, Vogelxo, Fortesta).

    ▪ Patch—A patch containing testosterone is put on an arm or the torso each night.

- Injections—Depo-Testosterone and testosterone enanthate are injected into the muscle or under the skin.

- Slow-Release Pellets—These pellets are implanted under the skin every 3 to 6 months.

- Nasal—This testosterone gel can be pumped into the nostril about three times daily and may prove to be a simpler, less invasive approach.

*Before beginning any treatment regimen, consult with your doctor for medical advice, risks and potential side effects.

Aversion Disorder (AD):

Aversion disorder, often referred to as **sexual aversion disorder**, is a condition characterized by an intense fear, disgust, or avoidance of sexual contact. Unlike a low libido or disinterest in sex, this condition involves a deep emotional or psychological reaction, where the mere thought of sexual activity triggers anxiety, panic, or even nausea. It can stem from various factors, such as past trauma, negative experiences with intimacy, cultural or religious conditioning, or unresolved psychological issues.

Potential Effects on Marriage:

Aversion disorder can significantly disrupt marital intimacy, leading to emotional and relational challenges. The affected partner may avoid sexual contact entirely, which can leave their spouse feeling rejected, undesired, or confused. Over time, this can create emotional distance, resentment, or frustration as sexual intimacy is often a vital expression of love and connection in marriage.

Potential Solutions:

- **Psychological:**

  o A therapist specializing in sexual health or a certified Christian counselor can help identify the root causes of the aversion and work toward resolution. Therapy may include trauma-focused techniques, cognitive-behavioral therapy (CBT), or gradual exposure to reduce anxiety.

o Honest, judgment-free conversations about feelings and fears can help the unaffected spouse understand the condition and offer support. Couples can discuss how to approach intimacy in ways that feel safe for both partners.

o Recognize that aversion disorder is not a rejection of the spouse but a deeply ingrained issue requiring time and effort to address. Patience can prevent additional strain on the relationship.

o Build emotional closeness through acts of affection, such as cuddling, holding hands, or spending quality time together. This can reduce pressure and strengthen the relationship foundation.

- **Behavioral:**

  o **Sensate Focus Therapy**—gradually reintroducing physical intimacy in a non-threatening way, starting with non-sexual touch and progressing to more intimate contact.

  o **Mindfulness-based practices**, such as deep breathing, meditation, or guided imagery, can help manage anxiety and create a sense of safety during intimate moments.

  o **Pelvic Floor Exercises**- The pelvic floor is a group of muscles and ligaments that support the bladder, uterus, rectum, and other pelvic organs. Tightening the pelvic floor muscles (as if stopping urine flow or preventing gas) or rapidly contracting and releasing the pelvic floor muscles in quick succession is beneficial for both men and women and is used to improve bladder control, enhance sexual function, and alleviate certain types of pelvic pain.

  o **Medical:** Hormonal imbalances, chronic pain conditions, or medication side effects (e.g., antidepressants) can contribute to sexual aversion. A doctor may recommend adjustments or treatments for these issues.

o **Lubricants**—Water-Based, Silicone-Based, and Oil-Based. Lubricants are a simple and effective way to reduce friction and enhance comfort during intercourse.

o **Water-Based Lubricants**: Gentle and widely compatible with condoms. Suitable for those with sensitive skin or allergies (e.g., Astroglide, KY Jelly).

o **Silicone-Based Lubricants**: Long-lasting and excellent for reducing friction. Excellent option for those experiencing severe dryness (e.g., Uberlube, Pjur).

o **Oil-Based Lubricants**: Natural oils like coconut oil can provide a soothing effect. However, you should avoid using this oil with latex condoms as they can degrade the material.

o **Anxiolytics or Antidepressants**—For individuals with anxiety or depression linked to sexual aversion, medications like selective serotonin reuptake inhibitors (SSRIs) may help manage symptoms**.**

o **Testosterone Therapy**—If low libido due to hormonal deficiency contributes to aversion, hormone replacement therapy may be considered.

o **Topical solutions** for discomfort and physical pain associated with sexual activity may prove to be helpful.

*Before beginning any treatment regimen, consult with your doctor for medical advice, risks and potential side effects.

2. **AROUSAL DISORDERS**

Erectile Disorder (ED):

Erectile Dysfunction is the consistent inability to achieve or maintain an erection firm enough for satisfactory sexual performance. While occasional difficulties are normal, persistent ED can indicate an underlying health condition or emotional challenge.

Potential Effects on Marriage:

This disorder is likely to create feelings of inadequacy where the husband may feel less masculine or desirable, while the wife may feel unattractive and unfulfilled. There may also be issues of avoidance of sexual activity and in some cases, this can lead to infidelity if the unfulfilled partner looks outside the marriage for fulfillment.

Potential Solutions:

- **Psychological**:

  o **Couples Counseling**—Helps spouses navigate the emotional and relational impact of ED..

  o **Sex Therapy**—A licensed sex therapist can provide strategies for maintaining intimacy without the pressure of penetration.

  o **Behavioral**: Weight loss, exercise, and reducing/eliminating any alcohol or tobacco use. Also, proper quality rest supports hormonal and physical health.

- **Medical**:

  o **Medication** (PDE 5 inhibitors, e.g., Viagra, Cialis, Levitra); The inhibitors work by relaxing muscles and increasing blood flow to specific areas of the body.

o **Testosterone Replacement Therapy**—To restore testosterone levels in the body.

o **Vacuum Erection Devices** (VED) —The VED creates an erection by using a vacuum pump to create suction. The erection is maintained by a tight band that's removed when the erection is complete. It usually takes about 30 seconds to 7 minutes to achieve an erection with this device.

o **Penile Injections**—With a very fine needle, medication is injected into the penis about 10 to 15 minutes before the man is ready to have an erection. The medication will cause the penis to swell without stimulation, but with foreplay or the spouse's desire to engage in sex, the penis is likely to become more erect.

o **Shockwave Therapy**—Low-intensity shockwaves can stimulate new blood vessel growth in some cases.

*Before beginning any treatment regimen, consult with your doctor for medical advice, risks and potential side effects.

Priapism:

A condition characterized by a prolonged and often painful erection that lasts longer than four hours and is not related to sexual arousal. It occurs when blood in the penis becomes trapped and is unable to drain, leading to tissue damage if left untreated.

Potential Effects on Marriage:

Priapism can deeply affect a marriage by disrupting physical intimacy, straining emotional connection, and diminishing overall quality of life. The pain and discomfort it causes during or after an episode can make sexual activity challenging or impossible, reducing intimacy. Additionally, frequent medical interventions or underlying conditions like sickle cell disease or medication side effects can add further stress to the relationship.

Potential Solutions:

- **Psychological:**

    o Create a safe space to work together to redefine intimacy in ways that strengthen connection without pressuring sexual performance.

- **Behavioral:**

    o Avoid substances like alcohol, recreational drugs, or overuse of ED medications, which can trigger priapism.

    o Stay hydrated and manage stress to improve overall health.

    o Pelvic Floor Therapy.

- **Medical:**

    o Address underlying causes like sickle cell disease, metabolic disorders, or blood clotting issues.

    o Adjust medications that may contribute to priapism, such as certain antidepressants or erectile dysfunction drugs.

    o In severe or recurrent cases, procedures like a shunt or penile prosthesis may be recommended to prevent future episodes or address erectile dysfunction.

*Before beginning any treatment regimen, consult with your doctor for medical advice, risks and potential side effects.

3. <u>ORGASMIC DISORDERS</u>

Premature Ejaculation (PME):

When ejaculation occurs with minimal sexual stimulation before or shortly after penetration and sooner than a man or his spouse desires (usually within 1 to 3 minutes of penetration).

Potential Effects on Marriage:

Premature ejaculation may make spouses feel less connected. There are also feelings of shame, frustration, and anger connected with performance anxiety. The feelings of dissatisfaction with the sexual encounter can also lead to avoidance.

Potential Solutions:

- **Psychological**: Cognitive Behavioral Therapy (CBT) to manage anxiety and cognitive distortions related to sex and restructure new thought patterns to improve mood, behaviors, and outcomes.

- **Behavioral**:

  o **Pelvic Floor** exercises or **Kegel** exercises help to improve blood circulation to the penis, enhancing the ability to achieve and maintain an erection through better muscle control.

  o This technique involves contracting the muscles at the base of the penis by contracting as if shortening it or stopping the flow of urine. Simultaneously, tighten the muscles around your anus as if stopping gas from passing.

  o The **"Start-stop" Method**—Intentionally stopping sexual stimulation just before reaching the point of orgasm which helps the body to delay ejaculation. After arousal slightly diminishes, the couple can resume sexual activity.

  o The **"Squeeze" Method**—After sex has begun and the desire to ejaculate is present, either spouse can squeeze the end of the penis just above the glans or tip until the urge to ejaculate passes.

  o **Mindfulness Techniques** may also prove to be helpful by allowing men to become aware of their physical sensations during sexual activity to reduce stress and anxiety which often contribute to ED. The techniques include promoting relaxation through focused breathing.

- **Medical**: There are several medications that can improve premature ejaculation; below are some to consider:

  o **Selective Serotonin Reuptake Inhibitors** (SSRIs) —This medication can improve premature ejaculation by increasing serotonin levels which act as a neurotransmitter that inhibits the ejaculation reflex allowing for longer sexual intercourse duration.

  o **Phosphodiesterase-5 Inhibitors (PDESIs)** —This medication is used to relax the muscles in the pelvic area, including those in the vas deferens, seminal vesicles, prostate, and urethra which can lead to a prolonged erection and potentially greater control over ejaculation.

  o **Tramadol**—It is also known for its pain-relieving effects, but it also may help with premature ejaculation. The medication has the ability to lengthen the amount of time between vaginal penetration and climax.

  o **Numbing Creams, Gels, and Spray**—These topical agents contain numbing medication (e.g., benzocaine, lidocaine, and prilocaine) to treat premature ejaculation. When applied to the penis 10 to 15 minutes before sex, they can reduce sensation and help delay ejaculation. These medications are often available without a prescription.

  o **Condoms**—Certain climax control condoms that contain numbing agents may decrease penile sensitivity which helps delay ejaculation. Condoms with thicker latex (e.g., Trojan Extended Pleasure and Durex Prolong) may also assist with PME.

*Before beginning any treatment regimen, consult with your doctor for medical advice, risks and potential side effects.

Delayed Ejaculation (DE):

Delayed ejaculation can present in a few ways: The inability to ejaculate during intercourse or at all. It may also present as delayed orgasm which requires excessive stimulation to ejaculate. Or it may present through the loss of erection which stops the intercourse altogether.

Potential Effects on Marriage:

Delayed ejaculation may lead to reduced sexual pleasure for both partners due to the prolonged time it takes to reach an orgasm. Going for extended periods doesn't necessarily equate to more pleasure and or satisfaction. Delayed ejaculation may mean prematurely ending the sexual encounter due to pain, tiredness, or irritation from the loss of erection or pleasure.

Potential Solutions:

- **Psychological:** Therapy that focuses on psychological contributors related to fear of intimacy, past trauma, relationship dynamics, and communication around sex.

- **Behavioral:**

  o Open communication and relaxation techniques. Sensate Focus Exercises.

  o Eliminating alcohol or any nonprescribed drug use.

  o I do not recommend masturbation or pornography use for delayed ejaculation because of the possible damaging effects it has on sexual response during partner sex. Men who employ this approach may be conditioning themselves to stimulus and arousal conditions that aren't likely to transfer well when they're with their wives.

- **Medical:** Address with your physician any potential side effects of the medication you may be taking or any medical conditions that may affect your sex life (diabetes, multiple sclerosis, spinal cord injuries, prostrate surgery, etc.).

*Before beginning any treatment regimen, consult with your doctor for medical advice, risks and potential side effects.

4. **PAIN DISORDERS**

Peyronie's Disease:
Development of fibrous scar tissue in the penis, causing painful erections or curvature. Symptoms include a noticeable bend or curve during an erection, pain during an erection or in a flaccid state, hardened lumps or a band of tissue under the skin, difficulty achieving or maintaining an erection due to compromised blood flow (erectile dysfunction), or a reduction in the length or girth of the penis.

Potential Effects on Marriage:
Men may experience feelings of inadequacy, embarrassment, or anxiety, leading to a loss of confidence. Wives may feel rejected, confused, or frustrated particularly if the condition is not openly discussed, leading to unspoken resentment, emotional distance, and dissatisfaction in the relationship.

Potential Solutions:
- **Psychological:**

  o Seek counseling to address self-esteem issues, anxiety performance, and any relationship strain.

  o A certified sex therapist can help couples navigate through challenges and discover new ways to maintain intimacy.

  o Support groups are good for connecting with others with similar issues that can offer coping strategies and support.

- **Behavioral:**

  o Open and honest communication about concerns to build understanding and intimacy.

  o Redefine physical intimacy by exploring forms of connection that do not rely on penetration, such as massages, kissing, or mutual stimulation.

  o Adopt a healthy diet and exercise to improve overall circulation and reduce inflammation.

  o Avoid smoking and alcohol consumption. Both substances have the potential to worsen symptoms or contribute to erectile dysfunction.

- **Medical:**

  o **Seek Medical Treatment:** Medical intervention can improve symptoms and restore sexual function.

  o Medications that break down scar tissue.

  o Oral medications can be considered but may not be as effective.

  o Injections (steroids) that reduce pain and curvature.

  o Surgery to remove scar tissue or for penile implants (in extreme cases).

- **Non-Surgical Treatments:**

  o Penile Traction Therapy (the use of devices that stretch the penis to reduce curvature).

  o Shockwave Therapy (the use of low-intensity shockwaves to improve blood flow and reduce scars).

Prostatitis:

Inflammation of the prostate can lead to pain during ejaculation. It can cause a range of symptoms, such as pain in the pelvic area, difficulty urinating, frequent urination, painful ejaculation, and in some cases, flu-like symptoms. Prostatitis can also disrupt daily life by affecting sleep and increasing stress levels.

Potential Effects on Marriage:

Prostatitis can significantly impact a marriage by introducing both physical and emotional challenges. Pain during intercourse or ejaculation may reduce sexual intimacy, while fatigue or chronic pain can drain a spouse's energy and mood, limiting physical closeness. Communication barriers can arise if couples avoid discussing the issue openly, leading to misunderstandings and feelings of isolation.

Potential Solutions:

- **Psychological:**

  o Create a safe space to talk about how prostatitis is affecting each other.

  o Seek individual or couples' counseling to address emotional and relational challenges.

- **Behavioral:**

  o Avoiding spicy foods, caffeine, and alcohol, which can aggravate symptoms.

  o Staying hydrated and practicing regular physical activity.

  o Focus on non-sexual physical affection, such as cuddling, holding hands, or massages, to maintain the connection.

  o Experiment with sexual activities that are less painful or taxing for the affected spouse.

- **Medical:**

  o Consult with a urologist to diagnose specifically which type of prostatitis you're encountering.

  o Antibiotics for bacterial prostatitis.

  o Alpha-blockers to relax the muscles in the prostate and bladder.

  o Anti-inflammatory medications to reduce pain and swelling.

  o *Before beginning any treatment regimen, consult with your doctor for medical advice, risks and potential side effects.

Specific Sexual Disorders for Women:

1. **DESIRE DISORDERS**

Female Sexual Interest/Arousal Disorder (FSIAD):

Female Sexual Interest/Arousal Disorder combines difficulties related to both sexual desire and arousal. The DSM-5 consolidated these issues into one diagnosis to reflect the interconnected nature of desire and arousal in women.

This disorder is defined by a lack of or significant reduction in sexual interest, arousal, initiation of sexual activity, pleasure, thoughts, and responsiveness to sexual stimulation (genital or non-genital) for at least 6 months, and is not better explained by another medical or psychological condition, substance use, or severe relationship distress (e.g., abuse) leading to distress.

Potential Effects on Marriage:

Female Sexual Interest/Arousal Disorder may leave husbands feeling rejected and undesired, leading to frustration and resentment over time. FSIAD is common (with estimates suggesting 40% of women being affected by it)—its occurrence can create emotional distance between spouses, weakening the marital bond. The couple may avoid discussing the issue due to embarrassment, fear of conflict, or worsening misunderstandings. This disorder may leave both spouses struggling with their self-worth and desirability. As sexual needs go unmet, the risk of seeking satisfaction outside the marriage increases.

Potential Solutions:

- **Psychological:**

  o Sensate Focus therapy and Cognitive Behavioral Therapy (CBT) to help couples rebuild intimacy.

  o Sex Therapy with a licensed sex therapist to address issues and explore options to overcome sexual concerns.

  o Encouraging open and honest communication regarding needs, desires, and concerns to build intimacy and trust.

- **Behavioral:** Mindfulness exercises, stress reduction, addressing issues of fatigue and depression. Getting proper exercise.

- **Medical:** Hormonal treatments: estrogen therapy, testosterone replacement therapy.

  o **Estrogen Therapy**—Estrogen plays an important role in sexual health and the presence of estrogen in women can increase vaginal lubrication and elasticity which reduce discomfort and pain during intercourse. Estrogen can improve mood and reduce symptoms of anxiety or depression.

    ▪ **Topical Forms**—Include creams (Sildenafil, Nitroglycerin, Femprox, etc.—some refer to these medications as Viagra for women). The creams are applied directly to the clitoris and external genital regions before sexual activity. They improve the blood flow to the genitals. Other topical forms include gels, rings, and suppositories.

    ▪ **Systemic Forms**—Include pills taken once daily at bedtime (Filbanserin), patches, and injections administered about 45 minutes prior to sexual activity (Bremelanotide).

o **Testosterone Replacement Therapy**—Testosterone is present in lower levels in women, but it is critical for sexual desire and arousal. Low levels of testosterone can contribute to FSIAD.

▪ **Topical Forms**—Include creams and gels.

▪ **Systemic Forms**—Include patches and injections.

Hormone therapy is most effective when combined with other interventions such as counseling, sex therapy, stress reduction, and other behavioral techniques.

*Before beginning any treatment regimen, consult with your doctor for medical advice, risks and potential side effects.

2. ORGASMIC DISORDERS:

Female Orgasmic Disorder (FOD):

A condition where a woman experiences a persistent delay in or absence of orgasm, or has fewer or less intense orgasms, despite adequate sexual stimulation. This condition can occur across all sexual encounters (generalized) or in specific situations, and it may have physical, psychological, or relational roots.

- **Generalized:**
  In this form, a woman has trouble or an inability to achieve orgasm in every sexual situation, regardless of the type of stimulation, environment, or partner. This may indicate underlying physiological or psychological causes that consistently hinder orgasm.

- **Situational:**
  In this form, the difficulty with orgasm occurs only under certain conditions. For instance, a woman may be able to achieve orgasm

through certain types of stimulation but not during intercourse. Situational FOD often points to factors like partner dynamics, stress, or discomfort in specific settings.

Potential Effects on Marriage:

As with any sexual disorder, Female Orgasmic Disorder can have an adverse effect on a marriage, impacting both partners emotionally and relationally. Frustration and feelings of inadequacy often arise, with the woman potentially feeling self-conscious about her inability to achieve orgasm, while her spouse may struggle with a sense of failure in meeting her needs.

Potential Solutions:

- **Psychological:**

  o **Open Communication:** Honest, judgment-free conversations about feelings, expectations, and needs can help reduce misunderstandings and foster mutual support.

  o **Education and Awareness:** Understanding female anatomy and sexual response can be empowering. Resources like books, workshops, or counseling sessions with a sexual health professional can be helpful.

  o **Counseling and Therapy:** Working with a licensed therapist, especially one specializing in sexual health or couples' therapy, can address underlying emotional or psychological factors.

- **Behavioral:**

  o **Experimentation and Patience**: Couples can work together to explore different ways to foster arousal and intimacy, focusing on pleasure rather than performance. Taking the pressure off can make intimacy more enjoyable and fulfilling.

o **Focus on Emotional Intimacy:** Building trust and emotional closeness outside of the bedroom can create a foundation for a healthier sexual relationship. Activities like spending quality time together or sharing spiritual practices, such as prayer, can help.

- **Medical:**

  o **Medical Consultation**: Since FOD may have physical causes (e.g., hormonal imbalances, medication side effects, or underlying health issues), consulting a health-care provider is crucial for proper diagnosis and treatment.

3. **PAIN DISORDERS:**

Genito-Pelvic Pain/Penetration Disorder (GPPPD):

Genito-Pelvic Pain/Penetration Disorder refers to sexual disorders characterized by recurrent difficulties with vaginal penetration during intercourse. These difficulties include pain during penetration, fear or anxiety related to penetration, and involuntary pelvic floor muscle contractions. This disorder includes the former diagnoses of dyspareunia (genital pain that occurs before, during, or after intercourse) and vaginismus (involuntary vaginal muscle contractions that prevent vaginal penetration or make it painful).

Potential Effects on Marriage:

Genito-Pelvic Pain/Penetration Disorder in marriage can affect physical intimacy, emotional connection, and overall relationship satisfaction. Pain during intercourse creates diminished pleasure and leads to avoidance of intimacy. Instead of lovemaking being a time of closeness and connection, it's viewed as a source of stress and apprehension. A lack of sexual intimacy can cause dissatisfaction and unhappiness in the marriage. Emotional distance and dissatisfaction may increase the risk of infidelity.

Potential Solutions:

- **Psychological:** Couples' counseling to improve communication and to address the emotional effects of the disorder. Identify alternative ways to maintain intimacy without the pressure of intercourse (e.g., spending quality time together, massages, cuddling, etc.).

- **Behavioral:** Pelvic Floor exercises, pain management strategies.

- **Medical:** Hormonal therapy (Topical Estrogen which helps to alleviate pain associated with vaginal dryness). Consult a gynecologist to address any other underlying medical conditions (e.g., infections, hormonal imbalances, endometriosis, etc.).

*Before beginning any treatment regimen, consult with your doctor for medical advice, risks and potential side effects.

Genitourinary Syndrome of Menopause (GSM):

Genitourinary Syndrome of Menopause (GSM) is comprised of symptoms and changes that occur in the vaginal and urinary areas due to decreased estrogen levels during menopause. It affects about 50% of postmenopausal women and can significantly impact sexual intimacy and overall quality of life. GSM symptoms include vaginal dryness, burning or irritation, loss of elasticity, or pain during intercourse (dyspareunia). Urinary symptoms include increased frequency of urination, urinary tract infections (UTIs), and urinary incontinence. Other symptoms include reduced sexual desire or arousal due to discomfort and vaginal spotting or bleeding after intercourse.

Potential Effects on Marriage:

Genitourinary Syndrome of Menopause can significantly impact a couple's intimacy and communication, creating a range of challenges that ripple through their relationship. Physical discomfort or pain during intercourse often leads to a decrease in sexual activity, which can leave both partners feeling frustrated and disconnected as their physical bond diminishes. This physical struggle is often accompanied by emotional strain as women may experience feelings of inadequacy, embarrassment, or reduced confidence, while their partners might feel rejected or helpless in their attempts to offer support.

Menopause describes the stage of a woman's life when her menstrual periods stop permanently, and she can no longer get pregnant. A woman reaches menopause when she has not had a period or spotting for 12 months. The time leading up to menopause is called perimenopause.

Potential Solutions:

- **Psychological:**

  o Couples' Therapy or counseling that specializes in sexual health or marriage counseling to address emotional and relational challenges caused by GSM as well as recommend treatment options.

  o Open and honest communication between spouses. Couples need to create a safe space to discuss how the disorder is affecting the relationship and explore ways to address it together.

- **Behavioral: Includes exercise and lifestyle changes.**

  o Pelvic floor therapy can help strengthen vaginal and pelvic muscles, improving sexual comfort and urinary function.

  o Regular Exercise: Boosts blood circulation, which improves vaginal health and sexual function.

  o Healthy Diet: Include foods rich in phytoestrogens (like soy and flaxseed) and omega-3 fatty acids to support hormonal balance.

  o Hydration: Drinking water helps maintain overall tissue health.

- **Medical: Behavioral:**

  o Vaginal Moisturizers and Lubricants: Over-the-counter options can provide immediate relief from dryness and discomfort during intercourse.

    ▪ **Estrogen Therapy:**

      – Vaginal estrogen (creams, rings, or tablets) helps restore moisture and elasticity without significantly affecting systemic hormone levels.

      – Systemic hormone therapy may be an option for women with more generalized menopausal symptoms.

    ▪ **Non-Hormonal Treatments:**

      – DHEA vaginal inserts (prasterone) or oral medications like ospemifene can also improve vaginal health.

      – Laser Therapy: CO_2 or erbium laser treatments stimulate collagen production to restore vaginal tissue.

*Before beginning any treatment regimen, consult with your doctor for medical advice, risks and potential side effects.

Encouragement for Couples

Sexual disorders can challenge a couple's marital intimacy, but they also create opportunities for growth and deeper connection. As husband and wife, your role is to support and serve one another, helping each other grow into the fullest expression of who God designed you to be. Facing these challenges together with patience, compassion, and practical solutions is an act of service to your spouse and it promotes unity, resilience, and growth.

If you're navigating the challenges of sexual disorders in your marriage, it's important to remember that physical intimacy is not just about the act itself—it's about creating connection, trust, and love. Intimacy is a gift from God, designed to strengthen your bond and express love in a way that words often cannot. But when challenges arise, it's easy to feel frustrated, discouraged, or even disconnected from each other.

The key is to approach these moments with respect and a willingness to support one another. Be open about your feelings, listen without judgment, and work together to find solutions. Whether that means seeking medical help, adjusting expectations, or simply creating space to reconnect emotionally, the goal is to honor the purpose of intimacy in your marriage.

Remember, this is an opportunity to grow closer, not further apart. As you face these struggles with empathy and teamwork, you'll not only address the physical challenges but also deepen your emotional and spiritual bond. Ultimately, you will both reclaim the joy and closeness that intimacy brings as well as reflect the love and unity that God intends for His children.

Chapter Reflection

Emotional and sexual intimacy are deeply interconnected in a marriage, each enhancing the other. Emotional intimacy, built on trust, vulnerability, and shared experiences, forms the foundation for a strong relationship. It involves not just expressing needs but also showing up for each other through everyday moments. When emotional intimacy is nurtured, it creates a safe space for deeper connection and love.

Sexual intimacy, far beyond a physical act, becomes a powerful expression of this emotional bond. It reflects trust, love, and commitment, allowing both partners to feel seen and valued. When emotional intimacy is strong, sexual connection flows naturally, deepening the relationship and strengthening the union.

These two aspects of intimacy complement each other, with emotional closeness fueling sexual connection and vice versa. The key is intentionality—actively nurturing both emotional and sexual intimacy helps couples stay bonded, especially through challenging times. While sexual intimacy may fluctuate, emotional closeness keeps the relationship grounded and resilient.

Ultimately, emotional and sexual intimacy are holistic aspects of a healthy marriage. When both are prioritized and nurtured, couples create a deep, lasting bond, built on love, mutual respect, and shared vulnerability.

Howbeit, on occasion, there may be issues that arise and hinder emotional and sexual intimacy, particularly the presence of sexual disorders. Sexual disorders, such as erectile dysfunction, low libido, or pain during intercourse, can significantly hinder both emotional and sexual intimacy in a marriage. These conditions often lead to feelings of frustration, shame, and isolation, which can create barriers to open communication and emotional connection. When one partner struggles with sexual health, it can lead to a breakdown in trust and a lack of confidence, further complicating the relationship.

However, acknowledging these issues and seeking professional help is crucial for healing. Open, empathetic conversations about the challenges both partners face can help rebuild trust and intimacy. Understanding that sexual health is a shared responsibility and addressing it together strengthens the emotional bond, allowing couples to move past the limitations of sexual disorders and reconnect in both emotional and physical ways.

Ultimately, addressing sexual disorders with patience, empathy, and communication can restore and deepen the emotional and sexual intimacy that strengthens a marriage.

Prayer

Heavenly Father,

We come before You as a couple, seeking Your guidance, healing, and grace. We acknowledge that You are the creator of our bodies and the intimacy we share. Lord, we ask that You help us build a deeper emotional and sexual connection, one that reflects Your love, trust, and unity.

We recognize that there may be challenges we are facing, whether emotional or physical, that are hindering our intimacy. We ask for Your healing touch on any sexual disorders or struggles that have caused pain, frustration, or distance between us. Lord, restore our bodies and our hearts, bringing healing where there is hurt and renewal where there is weariness.

Grant us the strength to communicate openly and vulnerably with one another, to create a safe and loving space where we can express our needs, desires, and fears. Help us to be patient with each other as we navigate this journey, supporting and encouraging one another every step of the way.

We ask for Your wisdom to guide our actions, so that we may honor and respect each other's boundaries while growing in trust and affection. May our love be a reflection of Your love . . . pure, sacrificial, and unyielding!

In Jesus' name, Amen.

PART THREE

Strengthening Bonds

CHAPTER 7

The Wonders of Worship, Witnessing, and Working Together:
A Journey of Spiritual Growth for Couples

Imagine a couple standing on the edge of a vast desert, staring across an endless expanse of sand dunes stretching toward the horizon. One partner turns to the other and says, "This journey will be long, but I'm glad we're walking it together." Life, and especially marriage, can often feel like this scene: a mix of unknown challenges, joyful discoveries, and moments of exhaustion. However, when two people walk together in faith, that journey becomes one of purpose, resilience, and growth, fueled by a shared commitment to God and each other.

Spiritual growth isn't simply about individual faith—it's about uniting as a couple to create a shared relationship with God. When a couple actively seeks spiritual growth together, their love is transformed; it matures, deepens, and roots itself in a foundation that stands against life's storms. As Ecclesiastes 4:12 tells us, *"Though one may be overpowered, two can defend themselves. A cord of three strands is not quickly broken."* That "third strand," representing God, is what transforms a relationship from just two people struggling through life into a unified partnership grounded in divine love and purpose.

It is at this juncture that I invite you to explore spiritual growth not only for yourself, but also for the health, stability, and lasting joy of your marriage.

The Foundation of Spiritual Growth
Shared Beliefs and Values

"Unless the Lord builds the house, those who
build it labor in vain." (Psalm 127:1)

Take a moment to reflect on your relationship and ask yourself this question: *What foundation did we build our relationship upon?* If you're like most couples, you probably built your relationship on shared interests, mutual attraction, and, hopefully, a shared vision for the future. But what about faith? What role has faith played in your relationship's foundation?

Shared beliefs and values form the foundation of a strong and thriving marriage, shaping how couples navigate life's challenges, make decisions, and connect on a deeper level. When spouses align in their worldviews and priorities, unity flourishes, conflict reduces, and couples can create a shared vision for their relationship and family. This level of unity stems from spiritual, emotional, and social compatibility that leads to a mutually beneficial outcome for both spouses.

2 Corinthians 6:14 encourages believers not to be unequally yoked together with unbelievers: for what fellowship hath righteousness with unrighteousness? And what communion hath light with darkness? The idea of not being unequally yoked is based upon Deuteronomy 22:10, "You must not plow with an ox and a donkey harnessed together." This verse forbids yoking two animals of different sizes and strengths. The Greek word for yoke is "Zugos" which means to join or couple together, as in a physical yoke binding two animals.

When two animals were yoked together, the yoke helped them work in harmony, allowing them to accomplish much more than one could alone. However, if one moved faster or slower, the load would become unbalanced, placing constant strain and pressure on the smaller, weaker animal as it struggled to keep up. Instead of working together, the two would pull against each other, creating conflict. For the yoke to function effectively and ensure cooperation and balance, the animals needed to be similar in size and strength, enabling them to pull the load as a unified team.

When it comes to marital and spiritual growth, husbands and wives must carefully consider who they are yoked to. Who is on your team? Who are you pulling with, and who is pulling with you? Just as two incompatible animals cannot work together effectively, a spiritually minded person will inevitably move in a different direction from someone who is an unbeliever. Their values, goals, and perspectives are shaped by fundamentally different influences—one by God's Word and Spirit, and the other by worldly thinking.

When couples lack a shared spiritual foundation, tension and struggle are inevitable. Misalignment may show up when one spouse wants to attend church on Sunday, while the other prefers shopping or engaging in other activities. Similarly, one may feel called to serve fully in ministry, while the other chooses not to participate at all. This imbalance prevents the couple from moving forward in harmony, much like an unevenly yoked team of animals. For a marriage to thrive, both partners must share a spiritual stride, pulling in the same direction, and working toward the same destination.

A beautiful biblical example of this is Priscilla and Aquila, a Christian couple who built their lives and marriages on faith in Jesus. This husband-and-wife team is introduced in Acts 18 as co-laborers with Paul, risking their lives for the sake of the gospel. They opened their home for church meetings and strengthened believers wherever they went. The strength of Priscilla and Aquila's relationship was evident in their shared mission to spread the message of Christ.

In my marriage, Apostle and I have had the privilege of working together in ministry for 37 years: 12 years serving under our pastor and the past 25 years pastoring ourselves. We were both believers, both passionate about serving and helping others, and equally committed to the work of the Lord. Yet, even with such unity, our marriage faced attacks. However, because of our strong spiritual foundation and faith in God, we were able to weather the storms and glorify Him through our perseverance. Life was "lifing," and without our shared faith, those challenges could have easily become another source of conflict and division.

To build a foundation of shared faith, take time with your spouse to identify the beliefs and values that matter most to both of you. What do you believe about God? What is your purpose? How do you view family, finances, forgiveness, and love? These conversations may uncover differences, but that's not something to fear. Instead, exploring and understanding those differences can deepen your connection. Together, these discussions help you establish a clear spiritual foundation rooted in shared beliefs and values, creating a solid base for your marriage to grow and thrive.

Reflection Questions:

1. What role does faith currently play in your relationship?

2. How does your faith influence your actions, choices, and how you view each other?

Exercise:

Write a shared "Marital Mission Statement" for your relationship. Think about your hopes for each other and for the legacy of your marriage. What values and beliefs do you want to guide your life together?

Developing a Prayer Life Together

Prayer is a personal, spiritual practice where an individual communicates with God, typically involving praise, thanksgiving, confession, and requests. It is a way to express one's heart, seek guidance, deepen faith, and develop a relationship with God. Prayer can be spoken aloud, or it can be done in silence. It can be formal or informal and is often seen as a vital part of spiritual growth, helping individuals align their hearts and lives with God's will. Through prayer, people seek to connect with God, share their desires and struggles, and listen for divine wisdom and guidance.

Building a prayer life as a couple is one of the most powerful ways to deepen spiritual intimacy and unity in marriage. It begins with intentionality, making prayer a priority, and setting aside consistent times to seek God together. Whether it's a simple morning prayer or turning to God before major decisions, these shared moments lay a foundation for a Christ-centered relationship.

Prayer is the heartbeat of a relationship rooted in faith. It's where you bring your worries, hopes, and dreams to God together. Praying as a couple can feel awkward at first. As you openly declare your hopes or struggles, you may feel vulnerable in your spouse's presence. But that vulnerability is what you should aim for as prayer allows both you and your spouse to share a side of yourselves that words alone cannot fully express. James 5:16 reminds us to "confess your sins to each other and pray for each other so that you may be healed."

In Matthew 18:20, Jesus says, *"For where two or three gather in my name, there am I with them."* When you pray together as a couple, you're inviting God into the intimate space of your relationship. You're acknowledging that you need Him not only individually but together as a team.

It's important to remember that prayer isn't just about making requests, it's also a time to praise God and express gratitude for His blessings. Focusing on thankfulness shifts your perspective from the problems you're encountering to God's faithfulness, encouraging you to appreciate and celebrate the prayers that have been answered and the growth you see developing in your marriage.

In the marital covenant, it is vital that you pray for one another, as it demonstrates care for your spouse, and it fulfills the call to "carry each other's burdens" (Galatians 6:2). No one knows your spouse as well as you do. Your heart is in tune with their concerns, their desires, their weaknesses, and their secret pains. Instead of complaining about your spouse's shortcomings (and it's easy to do), stay mindful that God ordained your covenant and it's your job to cover them in prayer. As a helpmeet, it is your responsibility to intercede and stand in the gap for the spouse that you are serving. Keep your prayers simple and heartfelt, knowing God values sincerity over eloquence (Matthew 6:7). Over time, consistency will make prayer a natural part of your lives.

Scripture offers powerful guidance for prayer, grounding our words in God's truth. Passages like 1 Corinthians 13:4–7 provide rich material for prayer topics, describing the qualities of love:

> 4 "Love is patient and kind. Love is not jealous or boastful or proud
>
> 5 or rude. It does not demand its own way. It is not irritable, and it keeps no record of being wronged.
>
> 6 It does not rejoice about injustice but rejoices whenever the truth wins out.
>
> 7 Love never gives up, never loses faith, is always hopeful and endures through every circumstance" (NLT).

As we reflect on these love characteristics, we are reminded of our own shortcomings. Instead of allowing condemnation or shame to take hold, prayer gives us the opportunity to confront our weaknesses, hold one another accountable, and ultimately trust God to complete the work in and through us.

The Bible encourages believers to pray regularly and systematically, but there are special times in the lives of couples when spouses must touch and agree. These special moments play a significant role in building a strong prayer life for couples, serving as sacred milestones and anchors in their shared spiritual journey. These intentional moments allow couples to invite God into pivotal events, challenges, and celebrations, creating a deeper sense of unity, purpose, and connection in their marriage.

Life is full of significant milestones, like getting married, starting a new job, buying a home, welcoming a child, or embarking on a new season together. Taking the time to pray before these major moments creates a foundation of faith and invites God's guidance, blessing, and peace into the decisions ahead.

In 1993, Kav and I were just 23 years old, dreaming of owning a home of our own. At the time, I was unemployed, and Kav was working part-time for minimum wage at $3.35 an hour. Despite our inexperience and limited resources, we knew enough about God to bring our desires and petitions to Him in unified prayer. We asked the Lord to align our pursuits with His will, seeking a home that would bless us and glorify Him.

Not long after, two job opportunities came my way. Once again, we prayed for clarity, trusting God to guide us to the right decision. We chose the position we felt God was leading us toward, and just two days later, I was promoted. While we were praying, God was already working behind the scenes, providing exactly what we needed to pay off debts and close escrow. It was the prayers that alleviated anxieties and allowed us to find confidence in God's plan as we trusted His guidance, Proverbs 3: 5–6: "Trust in the Lord with all your heart . . . and He will make your paths straight.".

Through every step, before, during, and after the process, prayer brought us clarity, guidance, and confidence. At just 24 years old, we closed on our first home, and we are fully convinced that our unity in prayer was the foundation of this blessing. God's faithfulness met our faith, and He provided in ways we never could have imagined. Prayer during such milestones becomes a reminder that God is at the center of your marriage, steering your journey as you walk together. When couples recognize that divine intervention is available to them through unity and prayer, there will be nothing too small or too great for them to bring before God together.

Prayer should definitely be employed during moments of crisis. Every marriage will face trials, health challenges, financial strain, loss, or relational tension. These seasons can either draw couples closer together or drive them apart. Prayer becomes a lifeline during hardship, allowing couples to stand united before God rather than turning against each other. By interceding for one another and crying out to God for strength and wisdom, couples find resilience and hope, even when the path ahead seems uncertain.

It was the second year of our marriage when we found ourselves praying, sowing, and believing in God for a child. Our prayers were answered; we were finally pregnant, but the joy was quickly overshadowed by a difficult and complicated pregnancy. The next nine months were filled with challenges:

weekly blood tests to monitor my platelets, two bone marrow biopsies, and countless tears. Throughout it all, Kav and I prayed fervently and consistently for healing, a healthy baby, and a safe delivery.

On January 1, 1991, we received devastating news. The doctors told us that my life or the baby's could be at risk. If I delivered vaginally, the baby could suffer bleeding in the brain. If they performed a C-section, I could potentially hemorrhage to death because my platelet count was dangerously low. Faced with impossible odds, my husband and my mother turned to intense, unwavering prayer, asking God for a miracle.

That night, the Lord spoke to Kav, assuring him that our daughter would be born at 2 a.m. True to His word, on January 2, 1992, Taylor entered the world safely at exactly 2 a.m. Today, 33 years later, Taylor is healthy, thriving, and a constant reminder of God's faithfulness and the power of prayer.

When we bring our challenges, concerns, and petitions to the Lord in prayer, it protects us from anxiety and prevents us from becoming angry with God over the consequences of our own poor decisions. Proverbs 19:3 warns, "People ruin their lives by their own foolishness and then are angry at the Lord" (NLT). I'm always baffled by those who make decisions without consulting with the Lord and then they become angry with the outcome. Listen beloved, not every good idea is a "God idea." It is wise to seek God's guidance, allowing Him to lead you and spare you from costly mistakes that could affect your marriage and family.

Philippians 4:6–7 reminds us, "Do not be anxious about anything, but in every situation, by prayer and petition, with thanksgiving, present your requests to God. And the peace of God . . . will guard your hearts and minds in Christ Jesus." I decree that the very next time that you pray, that it will serve as a reminder that God is your refuge and that you are not fighting battles alone.

Anniversaries offer a wonderful opportunity to reflect on God's faithfulness throughout the years and recommit your marriage to Him. Taking time to pray together on this special day allows you to thank God for the growth, love, and strength He has provided and to ask for His continued guidance for the road ahead. Only you know the depths of your endurance and what you encountered over the past year. So, give God thanks that you're still together.

Allow the Lord to speak to you about the impending year and what He desires from you. How He desires you to better serve your spouse. Kav and I start each anniversary with a prayer of thanksgiving and gratitude for the journey we've shared, and we close it with a declaration for divine guidance and favor for the year ahead. We are mindful that it is the grace of God that has matured us, transformed us, and kept us each year. As we celebrate another year of matrimony, we also celebrate God's goodness and favor in our union.

To build a strong and enduring prayer life, couples must regularly reflect on their prayer habits and make adjustments as needed. Life seasons change, and so do the ways couples connect with God. Perhaps busyness has caused prayer to fall by the wayside, or maybe the focus has shifted to personal prayers instead of shared ones. Taking time to evaluate, asking questions like "How can we pray more consistently?" or "Are we including God in all aspects of our lives?" helps couples stay on track. Reflecting on answered prayers also fuels encouragement and deepens trust in God's faithfulness, as He continues to grow you, your spouse, and your marriage. (1 Thessalonians 5:16–18: "Rejoice always, pray continually, give thanks in all circumstances.")

In essence, these special prayer moments, whether it's praying before significant milestones, during tough trials, or on anniversaries, become sacred markers in a couple's spiritual journey. They remind you of how far God has brought you and to keep your hearts anchored in His faithfulness as you move forward. As couples intentionally prioritize prayer and take time to reflect on its power, they'll find their bond growing stronger, their faith deepening, and their marriage continually glorifying God through every season of life.

The Helpmeet, NOT the Hurt-me

Remember, you're called to be a helpmeet, not a hurt-me!

When it comes to prayer, couples may unintentionally hurt each other in ways that weaken spiritual intimacy and create distance in their marriage.

Understanding these pitfalls can help prevent unnecessary pain and even draw you closer in prayer. Here are some ways spouses can operate in the "Hurt-me" role.

One of the most significant ways spouses can hurt each other is by failing to make prayer a shared priority. When one spouse longs to pray together, but the other dismisses or avoids it, it can leave them feeling spiritually unsupported and alone. Have you considered what message you're sending when you refuse to pray with your spouse? This neglect can come across as indifference, weakening the sense of partnership and intimacy that prayer is meant to build.

However, forcing your spouse to pray is equally destructive. Yes, you should pray together but be patient with your spouse and their readiness to do so. Forcing or guilting your spouse into praying together may create resistance, leading the one spouse to view prayer as an obligation rather than a shared, joyful practice. Instead of promoting unity, this approach can create tension and resentment. True spiritual growth happens in an atmosphere of love and patience, not coercion.

Prayer should be a sacred act of love and unity, but it can become harmful when used as a tool for criticism or manipulation. For example, the spouse that prays out loud for God to "fix" the other person's faults or shortcomings, such as praying, "Lord, help my husband stop being so lazy" or "Help my wife learn to be more loving and less of a nag". While the intention may seem well-meaning, this approach shames the other person and turns prayer into a form of judgment. Instead of uniting the couple, it creates hurt, defensiveness, and resentment.

Be careful not to let offense take root. You may feel, "If I can't be transparent in prayer, then I just won't pray at all." But that's the wrong approach. If there are specific issues with your spouse's behavior, bring them to God during your private prayer time. However, choosing not to pray for your spouse at all is harmful. If no one else is praying for your partner, you should be the one to stand in the gap. Neglecting to pray for your spouse can make them feel as though their struggles, concerns, or dreams don't matter. Marriage is about "carrying each other's burdens" (Galatians 6:2), and failing to intercede for your spouse, especially during challenging times, can leave them feeling isolated and unsupported, as if they're carrying life's weight alone. Your prayers are a powerful act of love and partnership.

Another way we hurt our spouse is by criticizing their prayers. Prayer is deeply personal, and criticizing your spouse's style, words, or approach to prayer can cause unnecessary pain. Your partner's prayers may not be long; you may not think they're "deep enough" and you may even think their prayer is simple. But remember, God alone judges the heart, not you. Don't let the enemy use you to tear down your spouse by criticizing their vulnerability. Doing so can destroy their willingness to open up in prayer and rob you of the opportunity to experience them as they truly are.

Sometimes, couples may use prayer as a substitute for addressing real issues in the marriage. While it is essential to bring struggles to God in prayer, avoiding honest conversations with your spouse by saying, "I'll just pray about it," can feel dismissive. Healthy relationships require both spiritual connection and open communication. Prayer should complement these conversations, not replace them.

Anytime our actions tear down our spouse and bring a reproach on the kingdom, we are operating from a "Hurt-me" vs a "Helpmeet" stance. To avoid hurting your spouse through prayer, approach your shared spiritual life with humility, love, and understanding. Pray for one another with compassion, encourage each other's efforts, and create a safe space for vulnerability. Instead of focusing on faults, lift each other up in prayer, asking God to strengthen your marriage and help you both grow. As you build a foundation of grace and unity, prayer will become a powerful tool for connection rather than a source of division.

A Practical Prayer Exercise:

Set aside a few minutes each day to pray together. It doesn't have to be a long or elaborate prayer, but it should be meaningful. Take turns bringing specific requests to God: pray for each other's needs, your shared dreams, or the areas where you feel challenged.

For instance, consider praying for patience in moments of conflict, or strength during times of difficulty. As you share these requests, you'll develop a deeper empathy for each other and an openness to support each other in prayer. This simple practice has the potential to transform the way you connect and communicate, creating a safe space to discuss challenges and joys alike.

Another great opportunity for prayer is while riding together in the car. Instead of filling the time with music, videos, or phone activities, consider choosing prayer. Whenever Apostle and I are driving, one of us may feel prompted to pray. If other activities are happening, we simply lower the volume and focus on pressing forward in prayer. Don't feel like prayer time needs to be planned; allow the Holy Spirit to guide you as He brings people, places, and things to your spirit.

When a thought, reflection, or vision crosses your mind, take it as a prompt to pray. Whatever reason you're thinking along these lines, whether you fully understand the reason or not, pray. Know that your prayers are precious to God, rising like a sweet smell before His nostrils. In those moments, you are also activating heaven's power, as angels respond to the Word of God declared on earth (Psalm 103:20–21). Your prayers carry weight, and they set divine action into motion (Revelation 5:8, 8:3).

Prayer is one of your spiritual weapons, so don't underestimate its power.

Reflection Questions:

1. What areas of your relationship do you want to invite God's presence into more fully? Begin praying intentionally about these areas and keep track of the tangible progress you notice. Set aside uninterrupted time with your spouse to reflect on the growth you've seen and identify new prayer goals to pursue together.

2. Identify areas in your marriage that are stagnant or those in which you are not experiencing God's fullness. Search the Bible for Scriptures that address these areas, take these concerns to God in prayer, and listen for guidance.

Discovering God's Word Together

In today's fast-paced world, with countless distractions competing for our attention, making time to study the Bible together as a couple can feel challenging. Yet, it is precisely in these moments of focused reflection that we can find profound insights into our relationship and spiritual growth. The Bible is more than a set of rules and old stories—it is, in fact, a living, active guide that speaks directly to us today, revealing truths about love, forgiveness, and commitment. Here's why incorporating regular Bible study into your relationship can be transformative, and how you can overcome common obstacles to make it a consistent part of your lives.

Studying the Word Transforms the Mind

Studying the Bible together opens new ways to view your spouse and your relationship. When you read and reflect on the Word of God, you are exposed to divine wisdom that goes beyond human experience. The Bible provides practical guidance on loving one another in a way that's deeper than simple affection or emotion—it teaches true, selfless love (I Corinthians 13:4–7). Even passages like Galatians 5:22–23 often referred to as the "fruit of the Spirit," can have transformative effects when meditated upon. This passage describes the fruit of the spirit as love, joy, peace, longsuffering, gentleness, goodness, faith, meekness, and temperance: against such there is no law. When couples sit down to discuss what these attributes mean in the context of their own relationship, they can gain invaluable insights into how to treat and love each other better.

Instead of merely reading through passages of Scripture, try to make it personal by asking questions like:

- What does it mean to be longsuffering with each other?

- How can we show gentleness to one another, especially during times of stress or disagreement?

- What does gentleness look like in our interactions, and how can we grow in this area?

These questions, and the conversations they spark, can create a healthy space for sharing and understanding that goes beyond surface-level communication. By openly discussing what these qualities mean to each partner, couples can learn more about each other's hearts, struggles, and desires, leading to a more authentic connection.

Overcoming Challenges to Consistency

One of the biggest barriers to regular Bible study as a couple is finding the time and energy to sit down together. Life is busy with work, family, and personal commitments, and it can be easy to neglect the sacred space needed for spiritual growth. However, overcoming these challenges often begins with intentionality. Start small by setting a specific time each week to study together, even if it's just 15–20 minutes. Consider using sermon notes from your church Bible Study, devotional guides, audio Bible apps, or group studies to provide structure, feedback, and engagement.

It's also helpful to choose books of the Bible that are relevant to the current season of life you're in, or that address specific themes you feel called to explore. For example, if you are dealing with challenges in communication or trust, a study on the Book of Proverbs could provide practical insights. If you want to explore the meaning of faith in growing your relationship, Hebrews chapter 11 is an ideal choice. Taking turns reading and discussing each passage allows for a natural flow of sharing and receiving, creating a sacred time to grow together.

Building Unity and Strengthening Commitment

As couples study the Bible together, they begin to share an intimate understanding of one another's spiritual journey. This shared experience can deepen the emotional bond and cultivate a sense of unity that goes beyond mere romantic attraction. When both partners actively engage in the Word, they create a space of mutual respect and accountability. This kind of environment encourages open communication and trust because it is centered around God's own teachings of love and sacrifice.

Moreover, studying the Bible together builds resilience in the relationship. As you navigate difficult passages and reflect on challenging ideas, you will learn to face conflicts and issues with compassion and patience, following the example of Christ. This kind of consistent study provides a place to address concerns, seek guidance, and reconcile differences, drawing strength from God's promises and the wisdom of His word. It becomes easier to resolve issues because, together, you share the same faith, and you are seeking answers from something greater than your own understanding or feelings.

In a culture that often pressures us to measure success and love by trendy standards, a consistent and intentional Bible study will serve as a stabilizing force. It provides a refreshing break from the chaos of the world and the shallow values it often promotes.

By centering your relationship around the Word of God, you are cultivating a love that is deeper, more meaningful, and more enduring than anything you could find elsewhere. So, start small, stay consistent, and watch the power of the word of God come alive in your marriage.

Biblical Example:

Consider Mary and Joseph's journey as described in Matthew 1–2. Though their path was difficult, they leaned on God for strength and guidance, modeling how to persevere through trials as a couple.

Exercise:

Choose a Bible passage that resonates with both of you and reflect on it together. Discuss what it teaches about God, love, forgiveness, or service, and talk about how these lessons might apply to your relationship.

Serving Together

Serving together can take many forms, from participating in local church ministries to engaging in global mission trips. It may involve mentoring other couples, supporting vulnerable populations, or advocating for justice and peace. Whatever the form, the act of serving together not only benefits those being served but also nurtures the couple's own spiritual growth and unity.

Ecclesiastes 4:9–12 speaks to the strength found in partnership: "Two are better than one, because they have a good return for their labor: If either of them falls down, one can help the other up." When couples serve together, their combined skills, passions, and spiritual gifts enable them to accomplish more than they could individually. This joint service promotes a deeper connection and shared sense of purpose, aligning their actions with God's call to love and serve one another.

Consider the joy and fulfillment that come from making a tangible difference together. As you work side by side, your marriage becomes a living reflection of Christ's selfless love. Serving others together has a unique way of drawing couples closer, allowing you both to exercise empathy, humility, and compassion. Ruth and Boaz's story (Ruth 2–4) beautifully illustrates the power of service in a relationship. Ruth's unwavering faithfulness to her family and Boaz's generous spirit toward Ruth and her needs created a legacy of kindness, commitment, and purpose. Their acts of service went beyond personal benefit, leading to a lineage that would include King David and, ultimately, Jesus Christ. Their story reminds us that serving others can have lasting, far-reaching impacts, often in ways we may never fully see.

When couples choose to serve together, whether in their community, church, or even within their own family, they not only honor God but also nurture their marriage. These shared experiences of giving and helping others create a more meaningful connection, a sense of shared mission, and a tangible way to reflect the love of Christ to the world.

For the past 42 years, Apostle and I have had the privilege of serving the Lord together. Our journey began with simple acts of service, like helping clean the church and finding ways to lighten our pastor's workload. This extended to personally serving our leaders, creating space for them to prepare and deliver God's word effectively. These acts of service, though humble, were deeply rewarding because they allowed us to work side by side, united in purpose.

Couples may initially grapple with finding balance as they try to protect the bounds of their marriage. But this level of service and commitment didn't take away from our time together, it actually strengthened it. Serving together brought joy and a sense of purpose that made the work feel light, not burdensome. Our hearts were fully invested in helping wherever we could, and this shared dedication became a foundation for both our marriage and our faith. Looking back, we see how these small acts of service laid the groundwork for a lifetime of partnership in ministry and a deep bond rooted in a shared love for God.

Over the years, as we faithfully served in simple ways, the Lord began preparing us for greater responsibilities in ministry. Gradually, our service expanded to teaching, counseling, and encouraging those around us. Because we had already developed a heart for service, stepping into these more demanding roles felt natural and deeply meaningful.

One of the most profound realizations during this time was that as we helped others, we were also helping ourselves. Walking alongside people in their journeys allowed us to glean valuable lessons from their experiences, their triumphs, challenges, and even their struggles. The good, the bad, and the difficult moments we encountered became opportunities for us to grow in wisdom and compassion. In serving others, we found that God was simultaneously shaping us, strengthening our bond, and deepening our understanding of His grace and purpose.

Today, we faithfully serve God by dedicating our time, treasures, and talents to His kingdom. We've surrendered everything to His use—the finances He has entrusted to us, the education and experiences He has enabled us to acquire, and even the home He has provided for us. There is nothing we withhold from God, recognizing that all we have belongs to Him and is meant to glorify His name.

Our current assignment as senior pastors in the house of God is both a privilege and a profound responsibility. This role has drawn us closer not only as partners in ministry but also as spouses and friends. We've reached a place of spiritual unity where we are so attuned to one another that we move in harmony, as one. Serving together at this level has deepened our bond and strengthened our commitment to each other and to God's work.

However, serving at this level does come with its challenges. There will be moments when you may need to step back and take some personal time to process your thoughts and emotions, allowing space to address any struggles or concerns. Yet, the rewards of serving together far outweigh these difficulties.

To ensure a healthy balance, be intentional about managing your time and setting realistic expectations. Pay close attention to your spouse's overall well-being, making sure their physical, emotional, and spiritual needs are being met. Prioritizing open communication and mutual support will help you navigate the demands of service while growing a thriving relationship.

Exercise:

Consider volunteering at church or in your community or finding ways to serve each other in daily life. Simple acts like preparing a meal, running an errand, or offering a listening ear after a tough day demonstrate care and commitment. These small, consistent acts of service build trust and nurture emotional intimacy, showing your spouse that their needs and well-being are a priority. Your service toward one another will be the impetus you need for serving others outside the marriage.

As you seek opportunities to serve, prayerfully ask God to guide you toward areas where your unique gifts and talents can be used most effectively. Serving encompasses more than giving, it's also about growing in your personal walk with God and with others.

Chapter Reflection

A thriving marriage is built on a foundation of shared beliefs and values. When a husband and wife order their lives with God's Word, they create a partnership that reflects His divine design. Shared beliefs become the anchor that steadies a couple during life's storms, while shared values guide their decisions and priorities, ensuring their marriage remains rooted in faith and purpose.

One of the most powerful ways to deepen this foundation is through developing a prayer life together. Prayer unites hearts, opens communication with God, and invites His presence into the relationship. It is in these moments of vulnerability and humility before the Lord that couples experience deeper emotional and spiritual intimacy. By regularly praying together, couples build a spiritual bond that strengthens their unity and helps them face challenges with grace and confidence.

Being a helpmeet as God intended involves supporting and uplifting your spouse rather than causing harm through words or actions. It means being intentional about nurturing your partner's well-being and striving to meet their needs with love and understanding. A spouse who is a helpmeet creates an environment where both individuals feel valued and supported.

As couples grow in their walk with the Lord, it is necessary for them to discover the Word of God together to keep their marriage Christ-centered. When couples dive into Scripture as a team, they grow in their understanding of God's will and learn to apply His principles to their relationship. This shared exploration builds spiritual intimacy and provides a firm foundation for making wise decisions and navigating challenges together.

Through prayer, Scripture, mutual respect, and service, couples can cultivate a sacred union that reflects His love, grow in strength, and stand resilient through every season of life.

Prayer

Heavenly Father,

We come before You, grateful for the gift of marriage and the opportunity to reflect Your love through our union. Lord, help us to build a foundation rooted in shared beliefs and values that honor You. May Your Word guide our hearts and actions, emerging our lives with Your will.

Teach us to come together in prayer, seeking Your wisdom and strength as a couple. Draw us closer to You and to each other through moments of stillness in Your presence. Help us to become true helpmeets, supporting and uplifting one another with love, patience, and grace.

Lord, ignite a passion in us to discover Your Word together, finding strength and guidance in its truths. Use our partnership to serve others as we reflect Your light and love in all we do. May our acts of service deepen our connection and glorify You.

Bless our marriage, Father, with unity, joy, and peace that transcends life's challenges. May we always keep You at the center, growing in love for You and for each other.

In Jesus' name, we pray.

Amen.

CHAPTER 8

Finding Favor in Finances:
Navigating Financial Responsibilities

Navigating financial challenges is a common yet daunting aspect of married life that can test the strength and unity of a relationship. This chapter addresses God as the creator and owner of all things while emphasizing man's role as a steward of God's creation and his responsibility to oversee what has been placed in his care. It also addresses the importance of managing finances in a way that honors God and supports the health of the marriage. It provides practical counsel on budgeting, saving, and investing, while also emphasizing the significance of generosity and trusting in God's provision.

The Origin of Everything

"In the beginning, God created the heavens and the earth" (Genesis 1:1). These words are not just the opening lines of the Bible; they are the foundation of our faith, an affirmation of God's ultimate ownership over all that exists. Since God created the heavens and the earth and the fullness of all that it contains, He owns it. Creation proposes ownership. Everything that we see, touch, and experience belongs to Him. As the psalmist declares, "The earth is the Lord's, and the fullness thereof; the world, and they that dwell therein" (Psalm 24:1). Nothing we possess, enjoy, or hold in our hands is truly ours—it is a gift entrusted to us by God.

This perspective on ownership is not a subtle suggestion; it's an undeniable truth, woven throughout the Scriptures. In Psalm 89:11, we're reminded that "The heavens are yours, and the earth is yours; everything in the world is yours, you created it all." In the book of Job, God asks a profound question: "Who has given me anything that I need to pay back? Everything under heaven is mine." (Job 41:11). This is not just a poetic truth; it is the bedrock of a life lived in alignment with God.

Imagine standing on a grand estate, admiring the vast fields, the trees, and the mansion at its center. You marvel at its beauty, but you are also aware that it's not yours to own; you're a guest, a steward, responsible for respecting and caring for it. This is how God invites us to view the world and all that's in it. He is the owner—we are the stewards.

As I have grown in my walk with the Lord, this foundational truth about stewardship is what transformed the finances in my marriage and catapulted my husband and me into a new realm of financial freedom.

I remember so vividly the summer of 1999 when the Lord commissioned me to give my beautiful 1995 Lexus GS 350 to my sister. Let me provide a little context so you can understand the gravity of my perceived trauma (lol). Kavin and I had paid the final payment on the Lexus, and might I add, we took a lump sum of money from our savings account to free ourselves from this car debt.

The Lord had already begun dealing with me about increase and giving. I never had a problem giving or being generous as it was always my nature to give. It was the way my mother had raised me, and I found great joy in blessing others and sharing what the Lord had blessed me with. But I had never given at this level. I had given money, clothes, jewelry, food, furniture, my time, and even cars—but not a luxury car that I had barely driven and just paid off. This was a game-changer! Little did I know that this was also a test of my stewardship to see if I qualified for greater depending on how I responded.

The instructions were very clear "The next time your sister's car breaks down, give her the Lexus GS 350." That thing shook me. At that time, I was also driving a 1997 Pontiac Grand AM that I was still making payments on. My rationale was "Ok Lord, I don't mind giving my sister a car, but can I give her the Pontiac?" In my mind, I would keep the luxury vehicle that was debt-free, and I would allow my sister to take over the payments on the Pontiac. I thought this was fair as I would not be asking her for anything in return.

The Lord said loudly, "NO! I already told you which car to release." I tossed and turned. I prayed. I fasted. I consulted my husband. And the resolve was to release the Lexus. I went to Kavin and told him that the Lord was commissioning me to give the Lexus to our sister because she needed transportation. He said, "Do what the Lord told you and we will be fine." This was also a test for my marriage as this decision had the potential to divide my husband and me.

We were a young couple (both 29 years old and married for 10 years), but we were learning that we owned nothing. The house we purchased in 1994 belonged to God. The cars we purchased and were driving belonged to God. The furniture, the jewelry, the clothes, the money we had saved belonged to God. Even the children we gave birth to belonged to God.

When we got the revelation of this stewardship, the pressure of ownership diminished, and we started experiencing greater increase and financial stability. It became increasingly easy to release anything that was in our care because it was not ours to begin with.

This was more than just giving a car away. This was God freeing Kavin and me from materialism and things. That car represented our second most valuable possession (our home being the first). Now we were tasked to release it. We were to ask for nothing in exchange for the keys and the pink slip. My sister owed us nothing. The car was a gift from the Father, and He used Kavin and me to present it to her. After we obeyed God and released the car with no strings attached, we both experienced a freedom we had never felt before. We were now beholden to nothing but to our God. If we were enjoying anything in our care, it was because the Lord allowed us to have it until He instructed us to do something different with it. We looked at everything from the lens of a steward and we were under the direction of the owner. Whatever He chose to do with His possessions was His business and it was our responsibility to obey.

Our Covenant and Stewardship

In Genesis 17, God's covenant with Abraham illustrates the biblical principle of stewardship, highlighting our responsibility to manage and honor the gifts, promises, and tasks entrusted to us by God. This covenant relationship wasn't merely a one-sided reward for Abraham—it was a sacred agreement that required his active participation and commitment. God's words "Serve me faithfully and live a blameless life" reveal that blessings and responsibilities are intertwined. Abraham was not to passively receive blessings but to steward them responsibly by aligning his life with God's will.

In a broader sense, stewardship involves recognizing that all we have is ultimately from God and meant to be used in service to Him and others. Abraham's role in the covenant underscores this principle. He was to be a conduit for God's blessing to future generations, managing the relationship with integrity, obedience, and trust. The blessings he received were not for personal gain but were meant to be used in accordance with God's purpose, extending not just to his immediate descendants but also impacting nations and peoples beyond his lifetime.

Abraham's story demonstrates that stewardship is about actively caring for and multiplying what God entrusts to us—whether that's faith, resources, relationships, or influence. It requires a commitment to live according to God's instructions, acknowledging His sovereignty (as expressed in the name "El Shaddai," or "God Almighty") and the purpose He has for us. Abraham's obedience and trust were his means of stewarding the relationship; in return, God's faithfulness ensured that the blessings extended to his descendants.

In this covenant, we see that our role in managing God's promises requires humility, trust, and an ongoing commitment to faithful living. By understanding our role as stewards, we can better grasp the weight of our responsibilities and the impact of our actions on future generations, encouraging us to live lives that honor God and nurture the blessings He provides.

As stewards, we are called to walk in this covenant relationship, understanding that our blessings are contingent upon our obedience to God's will.

Like Abraham, we're invited into a life of faith and partnership with God, knowing that He is the source of every good thing.

In managing God's gifts, our role is to align with His will, seeking His wisdom and guidance in every decision. As we embrace our role as stewards, we release our grip on the material and find freedom in the spiritual—a freedom that brings us closer to God's heart and allows us to experience the joy of living as a trusted servant in His kingdom. God desires that we reflect His character in our actions, using His gifts not solely for personal benefit but to serve others and show compassion. In seeking His guidance, we learn to prioritize generosity over accumulation, mercy over self-interest, and service over self-promotion. Through this, we discover the joy that comes from being trusted servants in His kingdom, living out our purpose with intention and integrity.

The Foundation of Financial Freedom

I have ministered on several occasions on the importance of believers understanding their stewardship role in the earth and recognizing that God the Creator is the owner of all things. Having a proper perspective on finances is necessary for living a financially stable and prosperous life as it touches the very core of our earthly responsibilities and our relationship with God as the ultimate provider. God is the source of all provision—He is not a resource.

In Proverbs 19:3, we are warned, "People ruin their lives by their own foolishness and then are angry at the Lord." When we face financial struggles, it's often a consequence of trying to manage our resources apart from God's wisdom. All too often, believers place too much confidence in the material possessions, the marketplace, earthly managers, supervisors, and workplace structures with the hopes of gaining financial increase and promotions. We convince ourselves that we need more income, more time, or less debt to gain financial stability. But what we really need is faith in the written word of God and obedience to that very word. The word of God must be our substrata, our foundation, the very thing that we don't just hear, but also the conviction by which we live. We can rest assured that God's promises are true, and His Word is reliable.

> 10 "For as the rain comes down, and the snow from heaven, and returns not thither, but waters the earth, and makes it bring forth and bud, that it may give seed to the sower, and bread to the eater:
>
> 11 So shall my word be that goes forth out of my mouth: it shall not return unto me void, but it shall accomplish that which I please, and it shall prosper in the thing whereto I sent it" (Isaiah 55:10–11).

God desires our obedience to His word. It is our obedience to the word of God that demonstrates our faith and confidence in our Lord and Savior. When believers become doers and not hearers only, we will see God's best manifesting in our lives daily. James, the half-brother of Jesus writes a comprehensive account of faith and works and how these two components produce tangible increase (James 2:17–24).

> 17 So, you see, faith by itself isn't enough. Unless it produces good deeds, it is dead and useless.
>
> 18 Now someone may argue, "Some people have faith; others have good deeds." But I say, "How can you show me your faith if you don't have good deeds? I will show you my faith by my good deeds."
>
> 19 You say you have faith, for you believe that there is one God, Good for you! Even the demons believe this, and they tremble in terror.
>
> 20 How foolish! Can't you see that faith without good deeds is useless?
>
> 21 Don't you remember that our ancestor Abraham was shown to be right with God by his actions when he offered his son Isaac on the altar?
>
> 22 You see, his faith and his actions worked together. His actions made his faith complete.

23 And so it happened just as the Scriptures say: "Abraham believed God, and God counted him as righteous because of his faith." He was even called the friend of God.

24 So you see, we are shown to be right with God by what we do, not by faith alone.

It was this revelation that helped me. I couldn't declare that the Lord was my Jehovah Jireh, my provider, and yet refused to release some of the blessings He allowed me to enjoy for fear of not getting those things again. If I truly had faith that He was my provider, why would I be afraid to demonstrate this through my obedient giving? It wasn't that God was taking anything away from me, He was attempting to give me greater, but I had to be tested and trusted that greater things wouldn't overtake me and replace Him. He was testing my stewardship. He was also using me as a conduit of blessings and allowing someone else to see Him as their Jehovah Jireh by providing for their needs and using me to facilitate the blessing.

Isaiah 1:19 states, "If ye be willing and obedient, ye shall eat the good of the land: 20 But if you refuse and rebel, ye shall be devoured with the sword: for the mouth of the LORD hath spoken it."

Financial freedom doesn't begin with more money or less debt; it begins with a decision to trust God's Word as the foundation of our lives which leads to a transformed mindset. God owns everything (Psalm 24) and we own nothing—when we align ourselves with His truth, we experience the freedom that comes from living under His authority.

The Steward's Mindset

If we accept that God owns everything, then we must also accept that we own nothing. I know this can be an unsettling thought and it can be very difficult to embrace since our names are on the possessions we enjoy. But the reality is, our homes, cars, finances, and even our time and talents are ultimately the Lords. This realization calls us to a higher standard, a life of stewardship. A steward is someone entrusted with managing another's property, a person who cares for something that isn't theirs.

In Luke chapter 12, Jesus tells a parable about a steward assigned to care for his master's goods. "And the Lord replied, a faithful sensible servant is one to whom the master can give the responsibility of managing his other household servants and feeding them. If the master returns and finds that the servant has done a good job, there will be a reward. I tell you the truth, the master will put that servant in charge of all he owns." (Luke 12:42–44, NLT).

In this parable, the servant is reminded that he is a steward who is managing his Lord's possessions and because he or she is a servant, they have the responsibility to manage what has been placed in his or her care according to the owner's will, not for their own benefit. When we are faithful stewards, we don't get to tell God what we will and will not do with what He has placed in our care.

God who is so rich in mercy and kindness, allows His children to enjoy much of what He has entrusted to us. Therefore, He doesn't ask us to relinquish everything He's given, but He does ask us to remember that we're managing His assets. Our responsibility is to seek His guidance and to manage His gifts with integrity, faithfulness, and a spirit of generosity. When we lose sight of this truth, we begin to act as owners instead of stewards, clinging tightly to what we think belongs to us, forgetting that it's God's to begin with.

In 1 Chronicles 29, King David models proper stewardship and demonstrates what it looks like to give joyfully, understanding that everything he offered came from God's abundance. Preparing to build the temple, David and his leaders gave gold, silver, bronze, and precious stones, all offered freely and joyfully, recognizing that they were merely returning to God what was already His.

David's prayer in 1 Chronicles 29:14 captures the heart of true giving: "But who am I, and what is my people, that we should be able to offer so willingly after this sort? For all things come of thee, and of thine own have we given thee." David's joy in giving wasn't just because he had wealth—it was because he understood that everything he had was from God.

When we give, whether it's time, resources, or encouragement, we're not making a sacrifice, but rather acknowledging that everything in our lives flows from God. This perspective frees us from any sense of entitlement and enables us to give with humility, gratitude, and faith.

Beware of Forgetting the Giver

Human nature often leans toward self-sufficiency and pride, especially when we experience success and abundance. There is a strong tendency to view blessings as something we have earned through our own efforts, skill, or intelligence, rather than as gifts from God. This inclination to take ownership of God's blessings is a recurring theme throughout Scripture, and Deuteronomy 8 addresses this issue directly.

In Deuteronomy 8, Moses reminds the Israelites of God's faithfulness throughout their journey in the wilderness, providing for them with manna, water, and protection. Now, as they prepare to enter the Promised Land, a land of abundance and prosperity, Moses warns them of a significant danger: the tendency to forget the source of their blessings once they begin to prosper. God cautions them that when they settle in this land, build their homes, and see their flocks and crops flourish, they might be tempted to say, "My power and the might of my hand have gotten me this wealth" (Deuteronomy 8:17). This warning reflects a universal aspect of human nature: when we reach a place of comfort or security, we often forget the One who enabled us to get there.

Instead of falling into pride, the Israelites were instructed to remember the true source of their blessings: "It is He that giveth thee power to get wealth, that He may establish His covenant" (Deuteronomy 8:18). This verse emphasizes that God is the ultimate provider, giving not only the material blessings but also the ability, strength, and circumstances that allow prosperity. The purpose of this blessing, Moses explains, is not solely for personal gain or status but to fulfill God's covenant and further His purposes.

From a biblical perspective, this warning is crucial for us today. When we attribute success solely to our abilities or efforts, we overlook God's providence and His role in our lives. Pride and self-sufficiency can lead to a hardened heart, one that is less inclined to trust in God, seek His will, or show gratitude. By remembering that every blessing is ultimately from God, we remain humble, keep our dependence on Him, and see our resources as tools to fulfill His greater plan.

In practical terms, this reminder helps us approach life with gratitude, generosity, and a spirit of stewardship. Instead of clinging to wealth or viewing it as a personal accomplishment, we can honor God by using what He has given us to serve others, support His work, and align ourselves with His covenant promises. Deuteronomy 8 is, therefore, both a caution and an invitation to remember God as our provider and to use His blessings in ways that reflect His purpose and glory.

God knows that blessings, when mismanaged, can become a snare. When we start attributing our success to our own efforts, we slip into the role of owner rather than steward. The remedy for this is the attitude—an ongoing acknowledgment that all we possess comes from God.

Living as stewards changes our relationship with everything around us. We are no longer possessors but managers, grateful for what we're entrusted with and ready to share as God leads. This shift brings freedom and fulfillment, a deeper joy than any possession can bring.

Marital Unity in Finances

In today's society, an increasing number of Christian couples choose to keep their finances separate, managing their incomes, debts, and spending independently within the context of marriage. While this approach may seem practical for maintaining individual autonomy and personal accountability, it does not align with the biblical model of marital stewardship.

In Scripture, marriage is portrayed as a union of complete oneness, where two individuals are called to become "one flesh" (Genesis 2:24). This unity extends beyond physical and emotional bonds to encompass financial and material resources as well. Keeping finances separate can create barriers that hinder the unity, transparency, and mutual trust that God intended for marriage.

In a Christian marriage, financial stewardship is more than mere money management; it's an expression of trust, unity, and commitment to God's design. By joining resources, couples not only deepen their connection, but also reinforce their shared priorities, values, and goals.

From a Christian perspective, shared finances are essential in building unity and trust within marriage. Genesis 2:24 says, "a man leaves his father and mother and is united to his wife, and they become one flesh." This "one flesh" concept applies not just physically but relationally, emotionally, and financially. When couples manage money together, they reinforce their commitment to work as a team, respecting each other's input and goals.

Imagine a couple, Linda and Steve, who decide early on to pool their income and create a family budget. Rather than viewing their income as "his" and "hers," they treat it as "ours." Each month, they sit down together, pray, and discuss their financial goals and needs. By sharing finances, Linda and Steve experience financial peace and mutual respect, with each partner feeling included and valued.

Shared finances encourage transparency and unity. In contrast, when finances are kept separate, it often leads to misunderstanding, secrecy, and conflict over spending. By managing money together, Christian couples can practice open communication and develop mutual trust, aligning their finances with their values and goals as a couple.

Avoiding Debt in Marriage

The Bible consistently warns about the dangers of debt, as seen in Proverbs 22:7: "The borrower is slave to the lender." Debt can be a significant source of stress and bondage, often causing anxiety and placing strain on relationships. For Christian couples, avoiding debt means prioritizing financial freedom and trusting in God's provision rather than relying on credit or loans to meet needs or wants.

When Kavin and I married, we were two teenagers fresh out of high school. We had no immediate debt, but within a short span of time, we started accumulating credit cards. In my freshmen year of college, I remember walking down Bruin Walk where a slew of credit card offers were made available to me. After receiving my first card and becoming intoxicated with immediate gratification and delayed responsibility, what was a girl to do, but apply for more credit? It felt empowering at the time, like a rite of passage into adulthood. This was fine for a season until Kavin and I both had several credit cards and a limited amount of income to address the debt. We were now overextended and had to make some changes.

We both began reflecting on how debt weighed down our parents' marriage as well as the counsel we received from my mother about staying out of debt. There were several lessons that Mother would echo throughout the years that helped us to become balanced and financially stable. Things like saving up for major purchases instead of using credit. When using credit, we did not realize we were paying more for the purchase because each month we were carrying balances that incurred exorbitant interest. She told us if we needed a new car, consider opting for a reliable used vehicle within our budget rather than financing a brand-new model. Though it required discipline and patience, her counsel brought us peace and kept us from the financial and emotional burdens of debt.

In a society where debt is often considered a normal part of life, whether through credit cards, car loans, or mortgages, choosing a debt-free lifestyle requires intentionality and discipline. Many couples feel the pressure to keep up with societal expectations, which can lead to overspending and reliance on credit. I have counseled numerous couples overwhelmed by debt, often because they lacked the discipline to wait or they were influenced by a neighbor's new purchase, sparking a similar desire in them to buy something new. This pattern of impulsive spending and keeping up with others is common, especially in a culture that promotes immediate gratification and comparison.

When couples fall into the trap of spending to match others or fulfill short-term desires, they risk compromising their financial stability and creating unnecessary stress within their relationship. Recognizing these influences and learning to prioritize patience and intentional spending can be transformative. By shifting their focus to long-term goals and a spirit of contentment, couples can begin to reclaim control over their finances, avoid the pitfalls of debt, and build a financial foundation rooted in wisdom and stewardship.

As couples choose to live debt-free, they gain financial flexibility that allows them to respond to God's calling in ways that may not be possible with the constraints of debt. Without monthly repayment obligations, they can more freely allocate resources toward helping others, savings, as well as giving generously to ministry missions and visions. This freedom not only reduces stress and anxiety about finances, but it also provides a sense of empowerment and peace, encouraging couples to view their resources as tools for God's kingdom rather than personal gain.

Saving Responsibly as Good Stewards

Responsible saving is another critical aspect of financial stewardship. Proverbs 21:20 reminds us, "The wise store up choice food and olive oil, but fools gulp theirs down." Saving allows couples to be prepared for unexpected expenses, reducing stress and fostering security within the marriage. However, saving isn't merely about accumulating wealth—it's about being wise with God's resources, ensuring that a couple is prepared to meet future needs and respond to opportunities for service.

Listen beloved, saving responsibly is more than a financial strategy for Christian couples; it's a commitment to honoring God's provision and caring for the future, cultivating peace, trust, and wisdom in your marriage. A responsible approach to saving allows couples to meet unexpected expenses without experiencing financial panic, while reinforcing a sense of stability that blesses both their relationship and family. Saving is often seen as a practical necessity, but within a Christian marriage, it also holds spiritual significance as an act of stewardship, aligning with God's wisdom in preparing for what lies ahead. However, while saving is valuable, it must be approached with balance, recognizing that trust in God, not in financial security is what ultimately sustains us.

I didn't learn the discipline of saving in the early years of our marriage, and as a result, those years were marked by financial struggle, poor stewardship, and frequent arguments. Eventually, Kavin and I reached a point where we knew we had to make a change. We committed to setting aside a portion of each paycheck for emergencies and focused on paying off our credit cards, making the decision to stop using them altogether. It wasn't easy! This choice meant forgoing certain purchases and delaying gratification so we could steadily build our savings. But over time, as financial challenges arose, we no longer faced them with the same stress and anxiety—we were finally prepared to handle them with confidence and peace.

For Christian couples, peace goes beyond simply avoiding financial challenges—it's also about a deep, abiding confidence in God's unfailing faithfulness. True peace doesn't mean an absence of obstacles, but rather a profound assurance that God will provide and sustain them, no matter what may come. This peace grows out of an active, trusting relationship with God, where couples anchor their lives not in circumstances, but in their faith in His character. Financially, this translates into a lifestyle of intentional stewardship, where saving is viewed not as a matter of self-reliance but as a wise, faith-filled practice that honors God. By saving responsibly, couples embody a balanced approach to financial stability, taking prudent steps to prepare for the future while acknowledging that ultimate security comes from God, not just their bank account.

Balancing Trust in God and Financial Preparedness

While saving is essential, Christian couples must also guard against placing their ultimate security in money rather than in God. There's a delicate balance between preparing wisely and trusting fully in God's provision. When we focus solely on accumulating savings, we risk placing our faith in wealth, subtly believing that financial reserves alone are enough to protect us. But Scripture reminds us that wealth can be fleeting and unreliable. Proverbs 23:5 cautions, "Cast but a glance at riches, and they are gone, for they will surely sprout wings and fly off to the sky like an eagle."

True security, then, is not found in a bank account but in a relationship with God. Responsible saving is an expression of faithfulness, but it should not replace our dependence on God's constant provision. Christian couples are called to balance saving with a deep trust that God will continue to care for them, knowing that He is ultimately the source of all they have and will ever need. This mindset shifts the purpose of saving from self-reliance to one of stewardship and partnership with God.

Kavin and I have always prioritized tithing and sowing seeds, finding joy in supporting church ministries as we consider ourselves "kingdom investors." After enduring years of financial struggle, we are finally able to give as the Lord leads, and we look forward to sowing whatever amount He prompts. We understand deeply that everything we have accumulated comes from God, and we value every opportunity to partner with Him. By honoring God through our tithes and offerings, we believe He sees us as partners in His work, and we remind ourselves often that our savings and financial stability is a tool for God's use and not a source of ultimate personal security.

When we feel led to contribute a larger amount for kingdom purposes, we don't hesitate. Growing in faith has allowed us to give freely, trusting that God will continue to provide for our needs as we follow His direction. This reliance on God, rather than on our finances, has allowed us to witness His provision in unexpected ways, reinforcing our faith in His unending care. For us, giving isn't just about money—it's about demonstrating our trust in God, knowing that He is faithful to sustain us as we commit our resources to His kingdom.

When couples commit to saving while trusting God completely, they experience a deep sense of peace that comes from being wise and responsible with their money. This kind of financial approach helps them avoid the stress of living paycheck to paycheck or being overwhelmed by debt. It creates a stable foundation that strengthens their marriage and family. With this solid footing, they're also in a better position to answer God's call to give, whether it's supporting a ministry, helping someone in need, or contributing to their church's mission.

Furthermore, this disciplined approach to saving and trusting God frees them to be generous without the worry or hesitation that financial strain often brings. Instead of feeling anxious about the future, they are prepared and equipped to give joyfully and meaningfully, knowing their foundation is secure. Through this balance of faith and financial wisdom, couples find themselves able to serve others and share blessings, experiencing firsthand the rewards of generosity and partnership with God.

Biblical Couples Who Honored God Through Stewardship

Aquila and Priscilla

Aquila and Priscilla were a married couple in the New Testament who used their resources to support the early Christian church. As tentmakers, they worked alongside Paul, opening their home to him and hosting church gatherings (Acts 18:1–3). This generosity wasn't limited to Paul—they consistently welcomed believers and even instructed others, such as Apollos, in the faith (Acts 18:26). Their hospitality and willingness to use their home for ministry exemplify how couples can honor God with their possessions, providing a place of refuge, discipleship, and fellowship.

Abraham and Sarah

Though the Old Testament doesn't highlight specific financial transactions, Abraham and Sarah's lives demonstrate a commitment to honoring God with everything they had. When God called Abraham to leave his homeland

and trust Him for provision, Abraham obeyed without hesitation (Genesis 12:1–4). Throughout their journey, Abraham often acknowledged God's guidance and provision by building altars and offering sacrifices, demonstrating gratitude and devotion. Abraham's readiness to offer his beloved son Isaac in obedience to God's command (Genesis 22) also reflects a profound trust, and willingness to give up even his most treasured "possession" to honor God.

Boaz and Ruth

Boaz and Ruth's story is a beautiful example of stewardship and generosity. Boaz, a wealthy landowner, extended kindness and provision to Ruth, a foreign widow, by allowing her to glean in his fields and providing protection (Ruth 2:8–9). He went beyond legal requirements, treating her with compassion and generosity, eventually marrying her, and ensuring the lineage of Ruth's family. Their union produced descendants who would lead to King David and, ultimately, to Jesus (Ruth 4:13–17). Boaz and Ruth's story shows how honoring God through generous actions can have far-reaching blessings beyond the immediate.

Zacharias and Elizabeth

Zacharias and Elizabeth, the parents of John the Baptist, were known for their faithfulness and righteousness (Luke 1:5–6). Although they are not specifically noted for giving finances, they dedicated their greatest blessing—their son—to the Lord's service. Despite waiting many years for a child, when John was born, they raised him in a way that prepared him to fulfill his prophetic calling. Their faithfulness in honoring God through their family set a legacy that would prepare the way for Jesus Christ.

The Proverbs 31 Woman and Her Husband

While the Proverbs 31 woman is often seen as an individual, the passage also speaks to the unity and trust within her marriage. She and her husband work together in ways that honor God and bless their family. This woman is resourceful and hardworking, engaging in activities like buying land, planting vineyards, and creating goods to sell, all of which contribute to her household's stability (Proverbs 31:16–24). She is generous, caring for the poor and needy, while her husband praises her and trusts in her (Proverbs 31:11, 20, 28). Together, they embody a partnership that uses resources wisely, demonstrating how a couple's commitment to stewardship honors God.

These couples exemplify how generosity, faith, hospitality, and stewardship reflect a deep devotion to God. Whether through their finances, their home, or their greatest blessings, they used their resources to advance God's purposes, leaving a lasting impact for future generations.

Here are ten sound solutions for couples to achieve financial freedom, grounded in biblical principles:

1. **Tithing**:

Tithing is the practice of giving 10% of one's income to the church or to charitable causes and it is important for both financial and spiritual health. When couples commit to tithing, they enter a financial partnership with God, inviting His guidance and blessings into their financial lives.

In Malachi 3:8, the Bible asks a poignant question, "Will a man rob God? Yet ye have robbed me. But ye say, wherein have we robbed thee? In tithes and offerings. In this passage, God calls our withholding of tithes a robbery against Him. Although God allows us to steward a large portion of what He places in our care, tithing is not included in this. The tithe strictly belongs to God and if we do not release it, it disrupts our spiritual alignment and brings a curse as indicated in Malachi 3:9–10.

As you deepen your understanding of financial stewardship, it's essential to acknowledge that everything we have ultimately belongs to God. This truth lays the foundation for lasting financial health and spiritual fulfillment. Achieving true financial freedom and prosperity becomes challenging when God is excluded from the equation. Tithing represents a sacred partnership with God, where He entrusts you with 90% of your income while asking for 10% as His portion. In my experience, there's no better partner to have in life or finances. Commit to tithing today and step into a powerful partnership with God.

2. **Giving**:

Beyond the call to tithe, practicing generosity allows couples to cultivate a heart for giving that reflects God's abundant nature. As John 3:16 reminds us, "For God so loved the world that He gave His only begotten Son, that whosoever believes in Him should not perish, but have everlasting life." Love compels giving—while it's possible to give without loving, it's impossible to truly love without giving. A heart that genuinely loves God will give to the advancement of His Kingdom.

Practicing generosity also has a transformative effect on our financial mindset. When we give as God directs, we break free from the grip of materialism and demonstrate that our trust is in Him, not in earthly possessions. This kind of generosity allows us to become true channels of blessing, willing to release what we hold in obedience to His leading. It's not about evaluating whether the recipient needs or deserves it—it's about honoring God's ownership of all we have and His right to direct its use. By giving with open hands and obedient hearts, we show our faith in God's provision and our readiness to serve as stewards of His blessings.

God desires not only that we bless others but also that we fully enjoy the blessings He freely gives. In 1 Timothy 6:17, we are reminded: "Teach those who are rich in this world not to be proud and not to trust in their money, which is so unreliable. Their trust should be in God, who richly gives us all we need for our enjoyment." God's provision is intended for our joy, yet He calls us to hold these blessings with open hands. He invites us to appreciate what He provides while ensuring our trust remains in Him, not in material possessions or wealth.

Ultimately, our giving reflects a level of financial freedom, and it serves as a recognition of our faith in God to replenish whatever we have released. In 2 Corinthians 9:6–7, Paul reminds us that "whoever sows sparingly will also reap sparingly, and whoever sows bountifully will also reap bountifully . . . for God loves a cheerful giver." This principle lets us know that our harvest is in direct proportion to our giving. If we don't like the size of our harvest, we must evaluate the size of our seed. Moreover, Scripture encourages us to give cheerfully. By giving cheerfully and without compulsion, we imitate God's generosity, unlocking blessings that extend far beyond finances, but blessings of peace, purpose, and spiritual fulfillment.

When couples regularly give above and beyond their tithe, they build a stronger foundation of trust in God's faithfulness, preparing them to receive and steward His blessings in greater ways. This generous mindset frees the giver from a place of insufficiency to a position of financial supporter.

3. **Open Communication:**

Consistent, open dialogue about finances is vital for building a foundation of trust and partnership in marriage. Ephesians 4:25 encourages believers to "put away falsehood" and "speak truthfully to your neighbor," a principle that directly applies to financial discussions in marriage. By maintaining honest, transparent conversations about money, couples avoid the potential for misunderstandings, resentment, or secrecy to take root. When both spouses feel free to express their financial goals, concerns, and values, they create a financial partnership based on respect, understanding, and mutual support.

Open communication around finances also brings unity and clarity to decision-making, especially when faced with difficult choices like budgeting, saving, or making major purchases. Regular discussions provide the opportunity to work through financial differences and agree on shared goals, whether that involves managing debt, planning for future expenses, or determining giving priorities. This practice helps couples stay aligned with each other and God's principles for stewardship. With open, honest conversations, couples create a safe space to plan their finances together, strengthening their relationship and empowering them to honor God with their resources.

4. <u>Seeking Counsel</u>:

Consulting with trusted financial advisors or mentors who share your values is a wise practice that can greatly benefit a couple's financial journey. Proverbs 15:22 teaches, "Plans fail for lack of counsel, but with many advisors, they succeed." There is safety and wisdom that comes from the counsel of experienced others. By seeking counsel, couples gain a broader perspective on their financial decisions, avoid potential pitfalls, and learn best practices for managing their resources effectively. Working with advisors who respect your values and faith ensures that financial recommendations align with your commitment to honor God through stewardship.

Seeking wise counsel also promotes accountability and provides valuable insights that may be difficult to see from within the relationship alone. Financial mentors or advisors can offer practical advice on budgeting, investing, debt management, and long-term planning, equipping couples to make informed decisions that facilitate their goals and values. When couples regularly consult those with experience and godly wisdom, they create a safeguard against impulsive or poorly thought-out choices.

Apostle and I know this firsthand, having faced financial loss in the past due to ignorance and impulsive spending. If we had access to the type of counsel we now provide to others, we would be much further along in our journey. Seeking counsel not only strengthens financial stability but also reflects a spirit of humility and teachability. It's a powerful step toward faithful stewardship and lasting success.

5. <u>Budgeting Together</u>:

Creating a budget as a team is essential for building unity, accountability, and mutual respect within a marriage. Proverbs 21:5 reminds us, "The plans of the diligent lead to profit as surely as haste leads to poverty," emphasizing that wise planning is crucial to financial success. By sitting down together to establish a budget, both partners gain a clear understanding of their financial situation, agree on priorities, and work collaboratively toward their shared goals.

Both spouses should participate in the budgeting. Doing so takes away the pressure of maintaining the budget when temptations to spend are present. This intentional approach to budgeting promotes communication and transparency, helping to prevent misunderstandings and disagreements that can arise when finances are left unmanaged or unspoken.

Budgeting together also strengthens a couple's commitment to stewarding their resources in a way that honors God. When both spouses participate in planning their finances, they're more likely to stay aligned with each other and remain disciplined in managing expenses, savings, and giving. This joint effort ensures that both partners feel empowered and engaged in the couple's financial health, creating a foundation of trust and shared responsibility. Working together on a budget reinforces a sense of unity, helping couples balance their needs and desires with long-term goals while cultivating a financial approach grounded in diligence, integrity, and respect.

6. **Debt Reduction**:

Prioritizing debt repayment is a critical step for couples striving to achieve financial freedom and stewardship aligned with biblical principles. Romans 13:8 encourages believers to "owe no one anything, except to love each other," stressing that debt can be a burden that limits freedom and generosity. By focusing on debt reduction as a couple, spouses actively work to free themselves from financial obligations that can lead to stress and restrict their ability to serve others and respond to God's call. When debt repayment becomes a priority, couples move toward greater financial stability, creating a solid foundation that encourages peace, unity, and flexibility in managing future goals.

Creating a debt repayment plan together not only provides a clear roadmap but also boosts teamwork and accountability. This plan might involve listing all debts, determining repayment methods like the "snowball" (starting with the smallest debts) or "avalanche" (tackling the highest-interest debts first) approach, and establishing a realistic timeline. Getting out of debt is not easy, but doable when discipline is employed. It requires both spouses to be in agreement, pulling back from purchases that are not necessities in this season (e.g., eating out for lunch, new clothes, purchasing the latest gadgets, or buying things because they're on sale, etc.).

Working as a team helps couples make intentional financial choices, such as reducing unnecessary expenses and resisting new debt. This journey requires commitment and sacrifice, but as couples see their debt decrease, they also witness the rewards of discipline, unity, and shared purpose. Together, they can experience the joy of financial freedom and position themselves to be a greater blessing to others, honoring God through their shared journey of debt reduction and stewardship.

7. **Emergency Fund**:

Establishing an emergency fund is a key element of wise financial stewardship that allows couples to face unexpected expenses with peace and preparedness. Proverbs 22:3 states, "The prudent see danger and take refuge, but the simple keep going and pay the penalty." This verse emphasizes the wisdom of preparing for unforeseen challenges rather than leaving oneself vulnerable. An emergency fund—typically recommended to cover three to six months of essential living expenses—serves as a protective buffer, helping couples avoid falling into debt or financial strain when unexpected situations arise, such as medical bills, car repairs, or job loss.

Building an emergency fund together also strengthens a couple's sense of unity and shared responsibility. By working together to set aside money for emergencies, couples show commitment to long-term security and peace of mind. Saving for this fund might involve small sacrifices, such as cutting back on non-essential spending, but the peace and stability it provides are well worth the effort. An emergency fund allows couples to face unforeseen events without panic, strengthening their trust in one another and in God's provision. This proactive step reinforces a healthy financial foundation, giving couples the flexibility to navigate challenges confidently and continue honoring their financial priorities without being derailed by life's uncertainties.

8. **Spending Wisely**:

Practicing discernment in spending is essential for financial stability and freedom. Proverbs 22:7 cautions that "the borrower is slave to the lender," reminding us that unchecked spending and impulsive purchases can lead to debt and financial enslavement. Making conscious choices about spending helps couples avoid these pitfalls, empowering them to steward their resources wisely. By prioritizing needs over wants, they can align their finances with long-term goals, stay true to their values, and avoid the pressure and anxiety that often come with financial overextension.

Spending wisely doesn't mean a life of rigidity; rather, it's about developing the discipline to distinguish between immediate desires and genuine needs. For instance, a couple might choose to save for future goals or emergency funds rather than purchasing unnecessary items. This discipline builds resilience and yields to a sense of purpose in their financial decisions. When couples approach spending intentionally, they avoid the burden of debt, enjoy greater financial freedom, and are better positioned to be generous and responsive to God's calling. Wise spending allows couples to live with peace and confidence, knowing they are honoring God through responsible choices and are prepared for both present and future needs.

9. **Long-Term Planning**:

Setting long-term financial goals is crucial for building a secure and purpose-driven future. Proverbs 24:27 says, "Do your planning and prepare your fields before building your house." This verse highlights the importance of careful preparation and forethought, encouraging us to prioritize essential steps before diving into larger commitments. In a financial context, long-term planning helps couples establish a vision for their future, make informed decisions, and take meaningful steps toward achieving their dreams and responsibilities.

Creating long-term financial goals might include saving for retirement, planning for children's education, buying a home, or setting up a legacy fund to support ministry or charitable causes. These goals require intentionality and discipline, often involving short-term sacrifices for long-term gains. By setting these goals together, couples strengthen their partnership and ensure they're aligned in their financial values and aspirations. This unified approach to planning builds a foundation of mutual respect, allowing couples to look ahead with confidence. Long-term planning is not only a wise and practical approach to finances but also a way to honor God by stewarding resources carefully and positioning themselves to be a blessing to others for years to come.

Achieving financial freedom as a couple requires intentionality, discipline, and a commitment to principles rooted in faith. By prioritizing generosity, open communication, and wise counsel, couples strengthen their bond and align their finances with God's values. Jointly budgeting, focusing on debt reduction, and building an emergency fund foster a foundation of security and peace. Practicing discernment in spending and setting long-term financial goals allow couples to prepare responsibly for the future while remaining generous in the present. Together, these steps cultivate a financial partnership that honors God, empowers couples to serve others freely, and leads to lasting financial stability and unity.

May we live each day with the faith that God is the ultimate owner, embracing our role as stewards with humility, gratitude, and a heart open to God's direction. For in this role, we find the true riches of life, not in what we hold, but in the privilege of serving the One who holds everything.

10. **Protect Your Assets:**

Make sure you have proper insurance to protect you and your assets, because what's not protected will be stolen. Early in our marriage, Kav and I learned this lesson the hard way. During a relocation, we stored our furniture, wedding gifts, college books, and other valuable items in a storage unit. Naively, we didn't purchase insurance for the unit, underestimating the potential consequences. We viewed it as an unnecessary expense, failing to understand that the cost of insurance was small compared to the loss we'd face if something went wrong. Unfortunately, our storage unit was broken into, and we lost everything. What should have been a simple precaution turned into a painful and costly lesson.

This experience taught us a critical truth: the upfront expense of insurance pales in comparison to the devastating financial and emotional impact of losing irreplaceable possessions. Insurance is not just about protecting physical assets—it's about safeguarding your peace of mind. Think of it as an investment in your future stability, a tool to minimize risk and provide security in uncertain circumstances.

Protecting your assets extends beyond safeguarding physical possessions; it's about securing your financial future, health, and legacy. Health insurance and car insurance are essential components of this protection, but having the right amount of coverage and affordable deductibles is equally critical. Too often, people choose lower premiums without considering the out-of-pocket costs when claims arise, leaving them financially vulnerable in emergencies. It's worth taking the time to ensure your coverage aligns with your needs and that you're not sacrificing quality for a slightly lower monthly cost.

Equally important is life insurance, a safeguard not only for you but also for those you love. Securing life insurance early is one of the wisest decisions you can make for your family's peace of mind. It ensures that in the event of your passing, your loved ones are financially protected from burdens such as funeral costs, outstanding debts, or the loss of income. The sooner you secure life insurance, the more affordable it tends to be, particularly if you're in good health. Think of it as a gift of stability and security for your family during an emotionally difficult time.

However, financial stewardship doesn't stop at insurance. Estate planning takes this protection to the next level. If you have assets, whether it's a home, savings, or even sentimental items, creating an estate plan is essential. Without one, your family may face lengthy and costly probate court proceedings, leaving your assets vulnerable to disputes and your desires potentially unmet.

Whether it's home, auto, health, or even life insurance, each type plays a role in preserving what you've worked so hard to build. Without it, you leave yourself exposed to unexpected events like burglary, natural disasters, accidents, or illness that can derail your financial progress and create undue stress. While these conversations can feel uncomfortable, they are acts of love and responsibility. They show your commitment to stewardship over what God has entrusted to you and your dedication to protecting and providing for those you care about. Procrastinating on these matters can lead to unnecessary stress and hardship for your family later on.

Chapter Reflections

Marriage is a sacred covenant that encompasses every aspect of life, including our stewardship over the resources God entrusts to us. As stewards, we are called to honor God with our finances, recognizing that everything we have belongs to Him. This chapter explored how understanding our covenant with God shapes a faithful approach to managing money, cultivating unity, and preparing for the future.

The foundations of financial freedom begin with aligning our financial habits with biblical principles. A steward's mindset embraces the call to manage resources wisely, balancing contentment with diligence. It also develops a heart of gratitude, avoiding the temptation to focus solely on what we lack.

Scripture reminds us to be wary of forgetting the Giver when blessings abound. When we fail to acknowledge God as our provider, it can lead to misplaced priorities, financial strain, and even division within marriage. Gratitude and humility keep us centered on Him and united with each other.

Marital unity in finances is vital. When couples approach money with transparency, trust, and shared goals, it strengthens their bond. Communication and teamwork in financial decision-making help prevent misunderstandings and allow couples to support each other's dreams and responsibilities. Couples must also stay knowledgeable of the dangers of debt. Avoiding unnecessary debt honors God and promotes peace in marriage. Responsible saving, paired with wise spending, allows couples to prepare for emergencies and future needs without compromising their trust in God's provision.

Finally, balancing financial preparedness with faith reminds us to rely on God while practicing wise stewardship. Saving is not a lack of faith but a reflection of prudence and responsibility, as outlined in Proverbs. Trusting God as the ultimate provider enables couples to plan for the future without fear or anxiety. As stewards of God's gifts, let us view finances as a tool to glorify Him, care for our families, and bless others.

Prayer

Heavenly Father,

We come before You with gratitude for the many blessings You have entrusted to us. Thank You for the gift of marriage and the opportunity to steward our resources together in a way that honors You. Teach us to see all that we have as a reflection of Your goodness and guide us to use it wisely and faithfully.

Lord, we ask for unity in our financial decisions. Help us to communicate openly, trust each other fully, and pursue shared goals that strengthen our bond and glorify Your name. Protect our hearts from greed, fear, and selfishness, and give us the wisdom to avoid unnecessary debt while saving responsibly for the future.

Father, remind us to keep our eyes fixed on You, the ultimate Provider. May we never forget that all we have comes from Your hand. Cultivate in us a spirit of contentment, humility, and generosity, so that we may use our resources to bless others and further Your kingdom.

Help us to balance our trust in You with thoughtful preparation. Guide us to plan with diligence and faith, knowing that You are the One who sustains us through every season. When challenges arise, strengthen our trust in Your provision and enable us to rely on each other as partners in this sacred covenant.

Lord, may our finances be a tool for peace and unity in our marriage, not a source of division. Let our stewardship reflect our love for You and our desire to serve Your purpose. We offer our resources and our marriage back to You, trusting that You will bless and multiply all that we commit to Your care.

In Jesus' name, we pray, Amen.